THE JOY OF
SMALL THINGS

HANNAH JANE PARKINSON

THE JOY

OF

SMALL

THINGS

First published in the UK and the USA in 2021
by Guardian Faber

Guardian Faber is an imprint of Faber & Faber Ltd,
Bloomsbury House, 74–77 Great Russell Street,
London WC1B 3DA

Guardian is a registered trademark of
Guardian News & Media Ltd,
Kings Place, 90 York Way, London N1 9GU

Typeset by Faber & Faber Limited
Printed in the UK by CPI Group (UK) Ltd, Croydon, CR0 4YY

A CIP record for this book
is available from the British Library

ISBN 978–1–783–35235–7

2 4 6 8 10 9 7 5 3

To those who have brought me much joy

CONTENTS

PREFACE

You probably know J. B. Priestley best for his plays. In particular, *An Inspector Calls*. But he also wrote novels and scripts and invented a theory of time. (And, as I was piqued to discover, lived in the same house in Highgate, north London, that was once home to Coleridge and, also, Kate Moss.)

But I like him best for his book, *Delight*: a collection of short essays on the things, people, places and feelings that delighted Priestley most; a rebuttal to his reputation as a life-long curmudgeon. *See, I like all this stuff!* This stuff included: fountains; cancelling plans in order to stay in (very relatable); reading about awful weather when tucked up in bed.

I had this book pressed into my hands by someone during an unsteady period and it helped pick the lint off my jacket, straighten my lapels and push me out into the world again. It helped me appreciate my own pockets of pleasure: the swirling sounds of an eight-minute end-of-album track, the route of a bus newly taken, a reinvigorating cold-water swim.

Back in 2018, times seemed particularly turbulent (little did I know what was to come) – the high-frequency bickering of social media; each day a Trumpism plumbing new depths; the quagmire of Brexit 'negotiations'. I found myself reaching for Priestley's delights once more. He found his in 1949, when the national mood was far from buoyant – a postwar period of rationing and an austerity drive close to the one we were then experiencing. I figured that if this grouchy Yorkshireman could take the time to sit down and document his everyday exultations, then I, someone whose default is a sort of droll cynicism, could do the same, no matter the fraying edges of the world around me. No matter the global, macro snafus, or the quotidian, quiet furies (the headphoneless music listeners, the reply-all emails, the cash-only bars).

These columns became my attempt to present the reader with the flowers in a tangle of weeds, the lilac of the gloaming, the most comfortable ever tread of a shoe. Inspiration to get us all through the day, without the need to text a friend a gif of a burning dumpster or to empathise with Edvard Munch's *The Scream*.

THE PERFECT
DRESSING GOWN

One of my favourite words in the world, aside from the German for armbands (*Schwimmflügel*, literally swimming wings), is the Russian word *halatnost*, which means dressing-gownness. This beautiful word was bestowed on the Russian people by Ivan Goncharov in *Oblomov*, Tolstoy's favourite book.

The word has come to mean negligence, but archaically (the novel was published in 1859), *halatnost* equalled lazing around reading the papers on a weekend, mooching about the house, doing not much at all. Maybe a touch of ennui, a lot of daydreaming. The life of the robed gentry: Oblomov is a nobleman who fails to move from his bedroom in the first fifty pages of Goncharov's book.

The *halat* in *halatnost* is all important. Halat: dressing gown. One makes big decisions in life: to have kids or not, where to put down roots. But up there, frankly, is finding the perfect dressing gown. Or, if you're northern and of a certain age, housecoat. If you're literal minded, a bathrobe – but we all know that's limiting its potential.

Give me a big, fluffy dressing gown that's like cuddling in a cloud or bathing in marshmallow. A dressing gown with a belt that wraps around you three times for safety. One with deep pockets in which to hold the world's minutiae (and, at

Christmas, After Eight wrappers). A dressing gown with a hood that makes you feel you could fight the world and win. A salmon- coloured robe in which to read the FT. A floor-length white one that reminds you of glorious sex in expensive hotels. Or a too-small, bobbled dressing gown – Liverpool FC red – that you wore when watching the *Match of the Day* repeat at the crack of dawn. An embossed smoking jacket, with matching slippers, sitting on a Chesterfield, with a roaring fire and a brandy. A satin kimono for summer, which begs to belong to someone who wears sexier nightwear.

When most people think of an 'investment piece', they think Mulberry handbag, Burberry scarf. I am thinking: dressing gown (but also Burberry scarf). A good dressing gown lasts decades, like a habit. One of the first written mentions of a dressing gown was in the 1660s diaries of Samuel Pepys ('my new gowne of purple shagg, trimmed with gold, very handsome'). Pepys knew.

When I found the perfect dressing gown, I am sorry to report it was from Soho Home, the homeware offshoot of Soho House. It was £65, but worth every penny. I could have spent £65 on a night out I didn't remember and then not had a dressing gown to recover in the next morning. I made the correct choice.

Some of the Worst People (specifically, men) have tried to bring the dressing gown down (Hefner, Trump, Weinstein), but I won't allow it. In the current state of the world, it's reassuring to know I have what is basically a comfort blanket with sleeves on the back of my bedroom door.

4

ALWAYS LOOK UP

I want to advise you something: always look up. Oh, the cornices and the eaves you might have missed! The kites in trees! The tall, handsome strangers with long, smooth necks. The pattern in the clouds that looks like a pig – or is it a bear? Or the outline of the UK, while the union lasts. The old brickwork adverts on the sides of Victorian buildings. The unexpectedly witty graffiti on the railway bridge. The ascending, spiralling, iron balustrades.

If you live in the country: look up for the stars and their constellations, or the book-lined studies of farmhouses, peeked through windows. If you live in the city: look up for the glass and the steel stretching higher and higher. I even like the Shard. If you're abroad and walking through dusty, narrow streets somewhere, look up to see the patterns of rugs thrown over balcony railings to air.

Looking down yields fewer rewards. The same feet you have known all your life, even if shod in spectacular shoes. Perhaps a gorgeous, reddening autumn leaf, but look overhead and there will be more. Looking up reveals new treasures and pleasures all the time.

It took me a few years to clock the Antony Gormley figure on top of Exeter College in Oxford. It took me riding on the top decks of buses (the best way) to notice multiple murals of butterflies in Camberwell, south London, before learning about the species of butterfly they all celebrated, originally native to the area (look up, too, to see actual butterflies). I focused on the café at the top of Mount Snowdon, scrambling up the scree as my bare knees became patterned with tiny stones, to will me on. I stumbled across a tree in the middle of London – in Hyde Park – home to glorious lime-green parakeets. They will swoop down and peck at slices of apples if you offer them. In Liverpool, where I am from, you will find another type of bird: the two copper Liver Birds, eighteen-feet tall with a wingspan of twenty-four feet, called Bertie and Bella, which top the Liver Building and watch over the city and the sea.

Look up in warehouses in Berlin, and marvel at the Bauhaus light fittings (if you're into that kind of thing, which I am). In Moscow, the famous ornate ceilings of subway stations are as much a tourist attraction as the Red Square. Lift your head to push on through a difficult run. Give your shoulder muscles a break from bending double over a phone when sitting at a desk or making an obstacle of yourself on pavements. Sometimes all it takes to really ground oneself is to tip one's head back and take in the vastness of the inescapable sky.

PLAYS WITHOUT
INTERVALS

I'll find myself in the office, at about 4 p.m., wondering whether I should go and see something at the theatre, looking online for availability that same evening, especially as the night draws darker and earlier. The good thing about going solo, which I mostly do, is that there is often a seat free, and discounted. I never plan ahead. I am lucky enough to live twenty minutes from the best productions in the world.

The true joy is a play without an interval. The television writer Steven Moffat once called for an end to intervals, which as an opinion earns a standing ovation from me. Intervals are rubbish: they disrupt the narrative; the toilet queues ribbon around the stairwells (I often just go to the men's: discuss); and my fellow audience members are excruciatingly slow in leaving and returning to their seats (I thought I saw Vince Cable at the theatre once, and then realised that every single person at the theatre looks like Vince Cable). Intervals are getting longer and longer, too, like Marvel films.

We need a break from intervals. We probably won't get one, because the venues need the revenue they bring in: the £5 thimbles of ice-cream, for example. Defenders will tell you that an interval is a good chance to discuss the performance, as though one would go to a book club halfway through reading a novel. They will talk about a chance to stretch the legs, as if we were on a 24-hour flight, at risk of deep-vein thrombosis.

Shakespeare's plays were written without intermissions. It is directors who insert them, running the risk of ruining them. I understand that sometimes a set change requires a delay in the action, and actors might enjoy a rest. But I would much rather stay in the dark, belief still suspended, than hang around in a sticky-floored lobby clutching a flat Coke (read: actually Pepsi) in a plastic cup.

Instead, give me, uninterrupted, a new world for the evening. Don't allow me the temptation to check my phone, forty-five minutes in, to have politics and work rush back into my head. Unwind me from scrolling. When I leave the building, I want the weather to have changed beyond all recognition. I want actors at the top of their craft, while I absorb every change in expression and movement. Give me a performance that changes my mood and my mind. Give me Pinter without the pause, and lines that inspire. Give me the lights down, and do not let them come up again until we rise to our feet as one.

KISSING

Do you remember the best kiss of your life? I imagine that you do. It's an evocative question – which is why a certain esteemed Saturday newspaper supplement (the *Guardian*) includes it in its regular Q&A feature.

An alternative query is: do you remember your first kiss? But that's not such a big deal. It is often fooling around with a friend, or at a pre-teen sleepover, or in a park somewhere, against railings, in the rain. Magical, too, of course. Special. Formative. But, for most people, probably not the greatest of their entire lives.

There aren't many things better than a great kiss. I am talking about romantic kissing – what we call (and here, a shudder) snogging. Such an ugly word for such a wonderful act. I once looked up the etymology of 'snogging' and the OED wasn't sure. Probably because nobody wanted to own up to it.

I don't think there is anything sexier than when you meet someone, before you have ever kissed, and your eyes keep mutually flickering to one another's lips with longing. I am not sure who came up with the idea of smooshing our faces together, but it's a good one. I couldn't date a person who was bad at kissing. Or, I suppose, more generously, bad at kissing with me. And I don't understand people who don't kiss during sex. It is such a fundamental part.

But a kiss can be pleasurable without sex, or the prospect of it. Some people are so good at kissing, or so compatible, that the kiss can be great even though you probably would not actually want to have sex with them. It works as its own shared, siloed intimacy.

There is no kissing off-the-rack. It's always specific to the situation, and the person. It can be fierce, full-throttle. Or gentler, slower. Kissing at its best becomes a fluency, a poetry; the highest form of communication, a physical language.

The best kiss of my life? I don't even want to share it. It was a conversation, almost. And, in this instance, untranslatable.

FONTS

Right now you are reading the font Aldus LT Std chosen by my Faber editor and me. It's possible you don't care about this; but I very much do. (The difference between a font and a typeface is that a font is a specific iteration of a typeface. Bold, italic, size, etc, though I'm not a stickler for this, so I'll just use 'font' here.)

Fonts are a huge part of our lives, because words and numbers are. Even if you think you don't have a favourite font, I can assure you that you absolutely do. Even if you think there is no font that would cause you to cross a road or avoid eye contact on the bus, there is. We are wedded to fonts; they work their way into our hearts and minds by both stealth and design.

A few years ago Helvetica became so omnipresent that it was the subject of longform essays, an exhibition at MoMA and a hit documentary. American Airlines, Toyota and Nestlé all use versions of it. Somewhat traumatically, it has also been used by the UK government. That may well have been the final nail in the coffin, as Helvetica became victim to tall poppy syndrome. Does anybody associate Chris Grayling and Matt Hancock with cool? No.

On the corporate side of things, fonts inspire brand loyalty.

You'll notice that sometimes when companies change fonts, consumers revolt. Often the companies just give up and change back. Gap once attempted to switch from its established serif font to Helvetica on a drop-shadowed square, and it just ended up looking like the header for a school-project Word document. It reverted. Tropicana also backtracked.

Bibliophiles, and I am one, take a keen interest in cover designs, but also fonts used. Have you ever read a book and found the lettering infuriatingly dense, making it hard to follow? Or one whose showiness is distracting? Have you ever been browsing spines on a bookshop shelf and had one jump out at you amid a crowded section?

Fonts have different personalities, which is why you never see Comic Sans on a funeral notice. Or a railway arch graffitied in Times New Roman. Authoritarian regimes tend not to stylise in a font called High Jinkies. I will never not find it amusing that I can write something in Arial, hate it to my very core; then switch the font to EB Garamond and think: this is a masterpiece. A perfect example, I'm sure you'll agree, of the transformative power of fonts.

COVER VERSIONS

Cover versions are like white wines: they're either very good or horrid. Horrid ones include mediocre guys playing acoustic guitars, wearing waistcoats over T-shirts, butchering every song released in the last three decades. Or how about the instrumental 'samba' covers of chart toppers that play in coffee shops, on repeat.

Good covers, however, are truly transformative. They turn a song inside out in the manner of a reversible jacket: same structure, but something entirely fresh. You can wear it pop or jazz or dance or rock'n'roll. Listening to a favourite song in a different guise taps into alternative emotions.

Cross-genre covers are the best for this, where artists and styles are completely juxtaposed, and each version becomes a go-to pick for certain moods. Robyn has become known for her 'sad bangers', because she often manages to pack contrasting moods into a single song. But while her high-energy 'Dancing On My Own' is on my playlist for getting ready to go out, Kings of Leon did a slow version that is depressing as hell and great for a wallow. I also could not have foreseen Patti Smith doing Rihanna's 'Stay', but it works.

I've spent a lot of time rewatching Radio 1 Live Lounge sessions on YouTube, which produce charming covers imbued with a sense of fun – aided by A4 lyric sheets stuck to the studio floor underneath snaking wires. The Arctic Monkeys' version of Girls Aloud's 'Love Machine' never fails to cheer me up (as does their Glastonbury take on Shirley Bassey's 'Diamonds are Forever'). There's something lovely in witnessing diverse artists appreciate each other.

There are covers that have overtaken the popularity of the originals, so that listeners might mistake the song's origins. 'Respect', probably Aretha Franklin's signature song, is an Otis Redding track; he wrote and recorded it two years before Franklin in 1965. And would anyone really argue that Roberta Flack's 'First Time Ever I Saw Your Face' isn't the definitive version of that song, despite it originally being a folk number written by Ewan MacColl for his future wife, Peggy Seeger?

Amy Winehouse's vocals on Mark Ronson's 'Valerie' will always get me on my feet. The Zutons' original doesn't, nor is it meant to. Winehouse's version is even more successful as a cover because she doesn't change the pronouns, which turns the love song on its head and creates a whole new narrative. That's really the essence of why I love covers: I am a greedy person, and they offer a whole new slice of life.

ICE-CREAM VANS

I knew a girl once who was scared of ice-cream vans, which is almost as depressingly unfortunate as people who struggle with sunlight because they are photophobic (or feign photophobia as an excuse to wear sunglasses all of the time; I am on to you).

Imagine being a child and not liking ice-cream vans or, indeed, ice-cream. That's a real gut punch. Ice-cream vans, which are one of those pleasures that does not diminish with age (at least, not if you are me) are the kind of wholesome, analogue enterprise which has held its ground in our modern leisure time.

As a child I lived in a road that ended in a park ('dead-end' is such an ugly term, isn't it?) and this induced a certain anxiety that passing ice-cream vans would not make the effort to stop, judging reversal up a sloped hill too much of a faff. Often, this was an anxiety borne out. Peeking out of the window with the net-curtain pulled back, I would clutch two pound coins in my little hand, eager with anticipation, only to hear the sound of the jingle fade into the distance. Talk about devastating.

This did mean that the times the sound grew louder were extra special. The menu, at eye level, popping with bright colours and promising rocket shapes of ice, spiralled delights, a pink foot, layered cones with a bubble-gum surprise at the bottom. The ice-cream van menu, each time, was a bit like when my father had taken me to choose a puppy – extremely happy-making, but bittersweet in the knowledge I could only take home one.

Nowadays I get my ice-cream-van fix from stationary vehicles in parks, or at festivals. I love a Mr Whippy and I do not see the point of one unless going all in. All variations of sauce; chocolate flake; sprinkles. I was dismayed recently to learn from one seller that sprinkles have been banned for hygiene reasons – although he's the only person I have heard this from. So the rest of them are sort of . . . the Al Capones of the ice-cream world? I would not recommend following the example of one woman who hit the news in 2014 for *calling the police* when a van ran out (how do these people exist?).

Sure, I love a proper parlour as much as the next person – fancy gelato in Tuscan towns, affogato in restaurants – but nothing beats the scrappy feel of a van decorated in seemingly random cartoon decals.

If there's one occasional negative, it's the horror of queuing, gaining access to that glorious whipped treat, and then promptly dropping it on the ground. This happened to me not too long ago, aged thirty-one. All of a sudden, I was five years old again, trying to stop myself from bawling. But, hey, it's a classic and integral part of the ice-cream-van experience, isn't it?

CLEAN BEDDING

There is something more comforting than luxury spa trips, or even indulgent massages. Something that soothes bones, costs (almost) no money, boosts the mood and makes the nights softer and the mornings lighter. Fresh bedding: clean, taut sheets, plumped pillows, the crinkle of a rejuvenated duvet cover.

As an insomniac, I look to any possible positive source of influence for a good night's sleep. Exercise often doesn't cut it; neither does banishing caffeine. And I cannot tell you the number of lavender-scented candles I've bought. The one thing that does, occasionally, seem to help is a ceremonial changing of the bedding.

This isn't reward without effort. In the winter months, drying sheets slide from too-small radiators, or hang like brightly coloured ghosts from racks. Before I change my duvet cover, I am tempted to text friends to warn them that, if they don't hear from me for three days, they must send help. (Sometimes I have to clamber in; I have learned that I would be good at caving.) I am also not convinced one qualifies as an adult while still using fitted sheets. Pillowcases, meanwhile, are origami.

But, my god, it's worth it. There is nothing better than the satisfaction of smoothing the top sheet until wrinkle-free

– an experience I imagine akin to a painter shrinking their canvas or a labourer pushing a trowel across wet concrete.

Don't just take my word for it. Research shows – even that not commissioned by publicists for homeware companies – that clean bedding improves your sleep. A 2012 study by the US National Sleep Foundation found that 73 per cent of us sleep better on fresh sheets. (And also that our romantic lives improve.)

I am cynical about advertising, but the women I truly believe in (and they are always women) are those who act in the fabric softener and detergent ads, who bury their noses in their queen-size beds with all the abandon of a clubber hoovering up a massive line of cocaine. It's also true that different people's beds smell different according to the washing powder they use. This is a little like an olfactory version of Proust's madeleine: if you one day accidentally buy the same brand as the ex you never got over, you're screwed.

One of the best things about getting older and having one's own money is to upgrade on life's basics, to step on the second rung of comfort. This means I no longer have to make do with bobbled sheets from college days and a mismatched pillowcase that is too large – think bank card in an envelope.

The Hans Christian Andersen story 'The Princess and the Pea' saw his protagonist kipping on piles of mattresses and feather beds to test her royal sensitivity. I used to think: who would even have that much bedding to hand? But I know better now: the lure of a John Lewis sale and a two-for-one on laundry products is my new dream.

THE ALL-DAY
BREAKFAST

A lot of money and imagination has been expended on finding the perfect hangover cure: IV drips; glutathione supplements; smearing oneself in mint. Anecdotal experience vies with professional advice: 'hair of the dog (drinking more alcohol) does not help', the NHS website states in a chastising tone.

Really, we all know the perfect hangover cure. It doesn't involve anything intravenous, costs just £5 and is easily accessible: the Full English Breakfast. Or perhaps more accurately, the All Day Breakfast (affectionately abbreviated to ADB) because any breakfast that isn't served after 11 a.m. is hardly better than useless. What if one only crawled into bed at 9 a.m.?

However it appears on the menu, the breakfast has to abide by certain edicts. It must be hearty. It must have a revitalising slow rise of steam – like thermal springs in Nordic countries – but not be so hot as to be mouth-burning. It must be some combination of eggs, beans, hash browns (non-negotiable), toast, and for the non-vegetarians, sausages and bacon. Not black pudding, which should be illegal (I have a petition; I'll send you the link).

Some eateries have introduced 'artisan' options, which often include avocado (it has the texture of the final sliver of

a bar of soap: you're all mad). Sometimes halloumi and spinach are involved, which I will allow. But the basics are best. Beans should be overflowing to the point of almost dribbling down one's shirtsleeves; the excess mopped up with toast. Butter should be served warm, so it melts into the bread as liquid gold. It should not come as cold as a mortuary slab.

Breakfasts should be advertised on a plastic swinging board, blocking half the pavement, outside a traditional greasy spoon. They should not be served on a slice of wood. The price should be rounded to the whole pound. Five pounds, or six, or seven, but never £6.65. This is not in the spirit of the hangover breakfast, when one is fishing out change from a pocket of jeans thrown on and basic mathematics is beyond a still gin-soaked brain.

The hangover breakfast comes with a risk. An unsettled stomach can creep on. The face becomes clammy, while the triangles of toast transform into unclimbable peaks. I recommend sips of builder's tea, rather than the heart-shaking addition of coffee. And water, lots of it. If all goes according to plan, the hangover breakfast is a reversal of a day's fortunes.

PETTING CATS

I have a cat. He is called Miles. He is a rescue cat who languished in his cage because he was extremely shy and therefore no visitors bonded enough with him to give him a chance. Eventually I took him home, with a 'pet pack' I bought from the cattery. This included a 'food scoop', which was, in fact, just a plastic shot glass. Miles arrived in my flat and bolted under the desk and didn't come out for days. Then, in the dead of night, he bolted under the cooker, and didn't come out for . . . weeks.

Months later, Miles loves me. He does not love or trust anybody else, and still responds to the front door unlocking the same way he would to a firework. But I am allowed to pet him. He adores being petted. He does not like being groomed, which is a problem, because he has a Shakespearean ruff and furry britches. His fur knots like a cat's cradle. He likes petting, which has no practical purpose except his own comfort and pleasure.

That comfort and pleasure is as much mine as it is his. I like to rub his ears between my thumb and forefinger, as though it is a swatch of material I am considering for a reupholstery project. He likes it, too. I like pressing the little jellybean pads on the underside of his paws, cold to the touch after he trots in. He likes it, too. I like scratching under his chin, his purr vibrating against my fingers. He likes it, too.

There's a spot on his back that if scratched causes him to fall to the floor and roll over sideways, the kind of move an eccentric drama teacher would dream up. Sometimes I hold him like a baby and his big, gold eyes stare into mine, mildly pissed off. (Miles is a jet-black, long-haired cat. He strongly resembles an owl, facially.)

Everyone knows the joy of pets, otherwise we would not share our homes with these animals that brazenly claw at our favourite clothes, or tear through furniture, or poo up walls or whatever mischief they get up to from one day to the next. The ubiquity of emotional-support animals has now tipped into peacocks-on-planes absurdity, but owning pets, and stroking and cuddling them, has health benefits.

One 2017 Swedish study even found that the risk of heart attack was 11 per cent lower in pet owners. Puppies have been introduced to relax finals students at universities. Cats are said to gravitate towards dying patients in care homes, to comfort them in their final hours. And, without a doubt, burying my face in Miles's hot belly is just as effective as benzodiazepines. It's also possibly more addictive.

WINDOW SEATS

There's a scene in Kieślowski's *Three Colours Blue* (one of the greatest films of all time) where Juliette Binoche sits in a café, idly pouring coffee on her ice-cream, going through real heavy shit, and looks out of the window at a man on the street playing a recorder. Personally, I wouldn't be hugely thrilled at a man playing a recorder during a meditative moment, but it's the sort of unexpected vignette of humanity that sitting by the window affords. I don't understand having the option to sit at a window and not choosing it. Would you walk around with your eyes closed? Or sit in the dark? Do you watch television with it switched off?

The restaurant at the top of the North Tower of the World Trade Center was called Windows on the World. But all windows are windows on the world. Sometimes they're not great ones – as anyone privy to a neighbour's dressing routine can attest – but more often than not, sitting next to a window is the inspiration of painters and writers; a crash course in anthropology; a catalyst for a change in mood or reflection on, like, life.

It's a proscenium, where the arch is a peeling sash frame, or the scratched, plastic edges of an Airbus, or the little blue curtains of a first-class carriage. The things you see. The people, animals, happenings. With urban windows, the everyday cordiality: drivers and pedestrians thanking each other with nods and semaphore. Amazing outfits. Friends joshing each other. Or the opposite: annoying lads doing wheelies in the road, endangering themselves and everyone else, half a decade before they'll shake their heads about it all.

Train window seats reveal green and gold treasures for miles. Thoughts appear from fields and tumble from skies. That doesn't happen when you're looking at an open-and-closing malfunctioning toilet door or are buffeted by trolleys selling Mini Cheddars for £5. In a plane, sure, you have to disturb your seat neighbours once in a while – for a wee, to stave off DVT – but it's worth it, for the pointillist pastel houses of foreign lands; the expanse of seas and undulating rivers never swum.

The significances of window seats are well recognised. That's why film cuts include characters staring mournfully past droplets of rain on glass, or CEOs looking out from top-floor offices, their feet on desks. It is why we're all well versed in the Parisian flâneur, strolling the streets before sitting and observing. It's why you can easily imagine me writing this, right now, watching the shadows on the pavement, the sun warming the glass, my chin in my hand, head turning slowly back to the screen.

POCKETS

Pockets are a feminist issue. Pockets are a class issue. Dedicated histories have been written on pockets. Research has been conducted. I appreciate all of it, because I simply adore a pocket. Even Ötzi (born 3345 BCE), popularly known as the Iceman (so popular in fact that Brad Pitt got a tattoo of him), loved a pocket. In his case, to carry flint and dried tinder fungus. Pitt probably loves a pocket.

Women, too, love pockets. And yet, we are continually stifled. It is thought it was circa the seventeenth century when pockets began to be sewn into clothes. Men's clothes, that is, not women's. (Although the word 'pocket' is a reference to the pouches women wore around their waists.) Pocket inequality remains: a 2018 study by website The Pudding found that pockets on women's jeans were 48 per cent shorter and 6.5 per cent narrower than those on men's. Often, garments for women don't even have pockets. Worse is the trend for fake pockets. I don't know who invented this charade, but I wish them a life of standing barefoot on upturned plugs.

I was constantly chastised when growing up for never carrying a wallet or purse. I didn't see the point, when I could enjoy skipping about, arms free to climb trees, give high-fives or smoke. I continue to stuff the usual items into pockets: keys, phone, debit card – even though I always carry a rucksack.

But I think my real love of pockets comes from standing in meetings with both hands slipped into well-cut trouser pockets, thumbs out, pretending to be at least eight times more intelligent and mature than I actually am (see also: wearing polo necks). In the summer, this is flipped to standing in a park, hands tucked into the back pockets of denim shorts, pretending to be at least eight times cooler than I actually am.

Some actual pockets are as infuriating as fake ones. The tiny jean pocket, for example, which was originally meant for cowboys' watches. (Hence, 'pocket watch'.) If I use this at all, it is for change. Apparently, it is now known in the industry as a coin pocket, though in the past it's also been a match or ticket pocket.

It has also been called a 'condom pocket', a name popularised by a 2006 Levi's 501 advert, shot by Michel Gondry in moody black and white over a techno soundtrack. I don't tend to carry condoms in my pockets – mostly because I think any girlfriend might be bemused. But I will never tire of the freedom to carry basically everything else.

AUTUMN LEAVES

The colours of autumn are abundant: the cool blue of the sky, the silver frost on the grass, the fuchsia of an early sunset. But the true riches are the leaves. The deep reds; the fierce oranges. The ochre of those curled at the edges. The shrivelled ones; the pale yellow of fading bruises. The combination of these colours against those crisp skies is majestic.

While the adjustment from summer to autumn can be tough – the reacquaintance with relentless rain and walking home from work in darkness – the colours are a solace. Walking around parks in October conjures Vincent van Gogh's *Autumn Landscape With Four Trees* (1885); the sienna, veiny delights of Georgia O'Keeffe's *Autumn Leaves* (1924); Gustav Klimt's *Birch Forest I* (1902). But best of all, David Hockney's huge studies of *Woldgate Woods* (2006).

Without wishing to go full curmudgeon, something is lost in the dying art of kids jumping into piles of leaves, eschewed for the bleeps, vibrations and scrolling of tech. Kicking up carefully raked leaf hills to the dismay of sighing park rangers. Taking a rugby-style kick and watching them flutter down like confetti. Mittens swaying from bare clapping hands. Instead we have articles warning parents of ticks and scratches.

Autumn leaves smell good. The Cambridge Dictionary defines humus as: 'Dark earth made of organic material such as decayed leaves and plants.' There doesn't seem to be a specific word describing this scent, but there should. Humussy?

Also, leaves sound good. There is the delightful crinkling that finds its way into atmospheric television scenes where characters walk together, breaking up or coming together, with hands deep in wool coat pockets, breath visible.

They feel good: that twiddling of stems between agitated fingers. They can be useful, too. Slipped between the pages of a book to keep a place or, less poetically, to wipe shit off a shoe.

The Russians were especially good at autumn. Chekhov, for sure. 'Mingled with the autumnal smell of leaves, the gravestones and faded flowers breathed forgiveness, melancholy and peace,' he wrote. Pushkin: 'Autumn attracts me like a neglected girl among her sisters. And, to be quite honest, she is the only one that warms my heart.' I wouldn't disagree.

PRIVATE JOKES

I have a friend, Eleanor, with whom I share so many private jokes that if one of us were involved in a crime and the police impounded our phones, it would take Alan Turing-levels of expertise to decode our text conversations. Think Anne Lister's diaries, but with the cry-laugh emoji after every single sentence.

One of the strongest bonds people can have is a shared sense of humour. As someone who basically finds everything funny, I have multiple versions of this. Eleanor and I often share very dark jokes, but also run amok with absurdism. I can fire witticisms back and forth with my friend David like it's a Wimbledon final. With Tshepo, we reference our past shenanigans and shriek with delight. Every time we hang out we add another one to the canon.

Chris and I love each other so much that we rip each other to shreds most days and, along these lines, there is a long-running trope that he is a cuckold, because I am having an affair with his wife. The WhatsApp group I am in with my school friends is filled with quotes that only we can comprehend. I have a colleague whose office I slip into when she's not in it and put up posters. One time, it was just a huge blown-up photograph of myself.

These little-and-often gifts are as revitalising as a vast intake of breath. All I need to be cheered on a bad day is an unexpected screenshot landing in my inbox of something that only a friend, or a small group of friends, understands. This is usually followed by increasingly zoomed-in screenshots of the same thing, or quickly searched-and-sent variations on the theme. Spontaneity and repetition are key to keeping private jokes alive. Riffs are built upon like Led Zeppelin songs.

But it isn't imperative to have a long history with someone to share a private joke. Sometimes they are fleetingly possible with strangers. Many a time I have caught the eye of a fellow passenger or queue member when something hilarious has happened, two perfectly unknown-to-each-other individuals mutually stifling smirks. This is best when nobody else has cottoned on or others are too mature to find the situation amusing. (It perhaps shouldn't be funny when someone trips up . . . but it just is – sorry. Ditto spoonerisms at live events.)

I am not entirely sure why esoteric jokes and references make me so happy, given that I can also derive much joy from humour that goes viral worldwide. But I imagine it comes down to a close sense of community and belonging. 'You had to be there' goes the phrase, and god, it's just beautiful if you were.

PETRICHOR

There are times when we discover a word that maybe we didn't even realise we needed, but after we are inducted we'd feel lost without. One of these words for me is petrichor. The *Oxford English Dictionary* defines petrichor as: 'A pleasant, distinctive smell frequently accompanying the first rain after a long period of warm, dry weather in certain regions.'

I was incredibly pleased to alight on this word because it meant I could stop asking people whether they also thought 'rain smelled good'. This isn't among the weirdest things I have been known to ask, but it's also not particularly hinged as far as queries go.

The joy of petrichor is separate but connected to the other benefits of a heatwave ending: the regained ability to sleep without all four limbs sticking over the edge of the mattress; being able to read one's phone screen outside again. I love hot weather – I enjoy heatwaves, even if with side-guilt at what they augur for the planet. But, like a new friend who starts off fun and energetic but ends up relentless, there comes the moment when the charm wilts (and in this case, the garden) and relief cannot come soon enough.

Enter: petrichor. The science bit involves an oil, trapped under dry soil and rock during the hot weather, being released to the surface by moisture. For me, petrichor smells like renewal. It's the rain equivalent of throwing a big, soapy bucket of water across grubby paving stones. Or a dog emerging from a lake and shaking itself down ready for the next adventure. It signals birth, resetting, resumption.

The word was coined in 1964 by scientists in Australia. It comes from the Greek for stone, 'petra' and, rather brilliantly, the word 'ichor', which is used to describe the mythological blood of the gods. The released oil is thus the 'blood of the stone'.

The smell had already been identified and even utilised in India. There it was referred to as 'earth perfume' or *matti ka attar* and perfumers bottled the smell and added it to their creations. (Please don't ask me to explain how this was done; let's just call it magic).

It is said some people, but more often animals, can smell forthcoming rain. I don't have the ability to turn my nose upwards and sniff out the clouds' impending rupture. But when a summer sky greys and loud cracks of lightning and thunder begin, I know it won't be long before I'll be huffing the good stuff.

TECHNO MUSIC

I am often asked what sort of things help me with my mental health. I think people expect me to say walking, nature, swimming. All of those things do help, all of those things I do need, but also: techno music. People never expect techno.

I used to hate techno; would rather die than listen to it, until I was sober for a year. It seems somewhat paradoxical to give up booze and suddenly start hanging out on vodka-sticky dancefloors. But, just like an SSRI, mix a high BPM into my brain and my mood will lift.

There's a physical element to techno that is lacking in other genres. There is, of course, joy to be found in sliding across one's kitchen floor in socks, bellowing out pop lyrics into the handle of a broom; but just as the physicality of exercise takes one out of the mind, so does the bodily response to the thud, thud, thud of techno. The rattling of the ribcage; the beat of the music in your chest – as if you had the world's most muscular, obnoxious heart. There's no space for bad thoughts, doubt or worry when the senses are assailed.

One summer weekend I felt awful. I spent the entirety of Saturday in a duvet-cave. The banality of life, the relentlessness. Boris Johnson. On the Sunday, I dragged myself from bed, threw some stuff in a bag and set off to Wilderness festival.

A couple of years before I had been revived, Lazarus by way of lasers, dancing at 2 a.m. in the festival's Valley – a literal valley – green beams scanning the night sky, pushing through trees in the black. Again, this is not something I envisaged a few years ago: I'm a huge Girls Aloud fan. But from that valley full of noise, I progressed to the thump of industrial techno at the infamous Berghain in Berlin. The sweaty basements and repurposed gasholders of east London. Wilderness worked the next year, too. (And of course I did the wild swimming as well.)

They say routine is good for mental health, and techno is nothing if not routine. A ten-minute techno track is the embodiment of keeping going. And there are barely any lyrics to drag the mind to places it isn't helpful to go.

A bonus is that techno often takes place in the kind of Brutalist spaces or decrepit warehouses that sing to my soul, but it can be equally helpful throwing my hood up, putting in my earpods, and walking around at night listening to a playlist that smacks as my heels hit the pavement. Try it.

FOREIGN IDIOMS

A group of professionals that I have a particular respect for is translators. Those who work to bring us the speeches and press-conference utterances of foreign leaders (ideally avoiding geopolitical disasters by not making mistakes – though there have been some close calls); and literary translators responsible for gifting me the brilliant *Drive Your Plow Over the Bones of the Dead*, an International Man Booker prize winner by the Nobel Prize-winning Olga Tokarczuk (which itself includes a subplot about translating William Blake), or the poetry of Anna Akhmatova.

Some of the most crucial translations, though, are those of proverbs. Idioms, adages, aphorisms from languages all over the world. These must be handled with care, like family heirlooms passed from generation to generation. Oral stories and national myths, too.

I collect these phrases as some collect stamps. Italy, as you might expect, has many food-based idioms. To have one's 'eyes lined with ham' is to be blind to something obvious. In France, 'to pedal in the sauerkraut' means to go nowhere fast, or have difficulty finishing something. I loved this originally because I assumed it referred to the texture of sauerkraut. But I later learned that it apparently comes from early Tour de France races, when wagons picking up stragglers often featured ads for sauerkraut.

I enjoy seeing how human brains, across place, time and culture, will make the same observations. And comparing the different ways in which we come to express those same thoughts. For example, in English: 'A bad workman always blames his tools.' In Russian? The much more brutal: 'Don't blame a mirror for your ugly face.' Thanks, mate. In response to a sneeze, the English might say: 'God bless you.' Mongolians go the extra mile, with: 'God bless you and may your moustache grow like brushwood.'

Other idioms are so bizarre that they appeal for their sheer imaginative energy. Prevaricating in Latvian is 'to blow ducklings'. Which makes no sense and somehow seems unfair on ducks. In Croatian, 'what goes around comes around' becomes: 'The cat comes to the tiny door.' Again, what? Then again, my cat would be angry if his cat flap shrunk. So, maybe.

Given our global political landscape, the Swedish description of someone privileged, who hasn't had to work to get to a prominent position, that they have 'slid in on a shrimp sandwich', seems widely apt. But let's end on a positive note. 'It is better,' the Chinese proverb goes, 'to light a candle than curse the darkness.'

RECOVERING
FROM A COLD

This may seem a tiny thing, but it has huge ramifications for one's happiness – a bit like winning the cup final with a goal adjudicated by video referee to be a millimetre over the line.

I am talking about recovery after a cold. Recovery from any period of ill-health, but in particular, the tentative escape from the banality of a cold, or a virus, or even just being 'under the weather' – as though when we are well, we soar above the clouds.

Being sick is the pits. Here, I think men get a bad deal with accusations of man-flu, i.e. the idea that men treat a simple cold as though they are slowly dying of a flesh-eating disease at sea. The truth is, at the sniff of a sneeze, most of us turn into pathetic avatars of our usual selves. Otherwise we would not move seats the moment someone coughed. (I know there are mothers who could power through tuberculosis if it meant getting the kids to school on time, but these are superheroes, anomalous case studies.)

Sickness means a mountain range of tissues in the bed. It's the gripping fear that tributaries of snot, flowing like the Dart, will never stop, and that the pressure in one's head will never shrink back to normal. That the eyelids will stay puffed up, like the worst examples of surgery gone wrong found in 'real-life' magazines, for ever. That it is worth it to pay £7.99 for branded paracetamol from the corner shop rather than stagger the extra half-mile to the supermarket and pay just 99p for the generic sort – because every second not in bed feels like the frontline of a war.

And then, just when you resign yourself to a permanently chafed nose, something magical happens: you wake in the morning, and the nostrils are crusted and a slither of air has entered, light at the end of the tunnel. As the day goes on, it's as though you have broken to the surface, drunk with the sensation of not being weighed down by four extra pounds of mucus. You even consider going for a bite and a drink after work, because you might be able to taste again. Your deskmates, meanwhile, have stopped shooting you filthy looks; at any rate, the looks are now non-contagion related.

You instantly forget how to spell echinacea and catarrh. You will never, ever, take for granted again the cilia that protect against bacterial invaders; you will always give thanks for the lungs that work so diligently on your behalf; you will never lose your reinvigorated passion for a throat that does not tickle. Of course, like a New Year's resolution, this resolve lasts mere days. Quick enough, being well is just the baseline one doesn't think about. But god, that first day feels like a lottery win. To your health, then.

DOGS IN PARKS

They say dogs are man's best friend. This phrase amuses me because I enjoy the idea that we might carry our best friends under our arms; walk them on leads; throw frisbees at them which we expect them to catch in their mouths. Just once I want to walk in on my friend in the act of gnawing on a slipper.

I do not own a dog, but I do not need to, because every time I step out into the world, dogs are ever present. The glorious and uplifting thing about dogs is that, unless they are sick, or maltreated, or lonely, they are essentially always happy. Or at the very least, content; and these two things are often catching.

Many attempts at going for brooding walks have been wonderfully ruined by the sight of a smiling labrador, totally in love with the world – this blade of grass! That other dog! Oh my god, that bin! My own tail!

There is the something-for-everyone variation, even within breeds. I simply adore a miniature dachshund – the hot, low, satisfied bellies; the curious snouts; the ears like a freshly cut bob; the Malteser eyes; the seeming mid-air suspension during full-pelt running – but I could not choose between short-haired, long-haired, or the ones dappled with silver.

Last summer I saw a white dachshund and I have never doubled back so quickly in my life (and one time I swear I saw a clown driving down the Archway Road).

Too frequently I forget to ask an owner their own name, but not their dog's, while utterly absorbed in their canine companion. I ask people with adorable, unusual dogs, whether they get stopped a thousand times a day, like A-list celebrities. (Invariably, yes.) So many times I pass dogs much better dressed than I am. Whippets in cravats.

I am an equal-opportunity admirer when it comes to size. There isn't much more majestic than the golden waterfall of an Afghan hound's (natural) coat. When I was growing up, our neighbour had six. When I asked my mother about the veracity of my memory, she replied: 'Oh, there were eleven at one point.' Meanwhile, I met a pomsky not long ago, which is a cross between a pomeranian and a husky. It had ears taller than its body and paws that looked to account for 70 per cent of surface area.

I do worry about selective breeding, but then I worry about selective schools and plenty more besides. I will not deny myself the pleasure of a trotting pup, a bubble-gum pink tongue, a tight spiral tail. But I should stop now; for the cat is getting jealous.

PHONE CALLS

Everybody has a mobile phone. Or at least more than five billion of us do. And yet nobody makes phone calls any more. In fact, the under-thirties have been called Generation Mute, for their habit of refusing to accept incoming calls. A recent UK survey found that just 15 per cent of sixteen- to twenty-four-year-olds would choose phone calls as their favoured method of communication. I once read an article with the headline: 'If I get a phone call, I assume someone has died.'

I used to feel similarly, but recently my opinion has shifted, and I have come to appreciate phone calls the way I did during my school days: when I'd almost pull the landline phone out of its socket in a desperate attempt at privacy, wrapping the cord around my fingers and spending a solid two hours talking to friends I'd just spent the majority of the day with; staying on the line for so long that the screeching dial-up sounds of my sister attempting to get on the internet would repeatedly interrupt, while dinners cooled and congealed on the dining-room table.

In the days of bog-standard landline phones without displays, the phone ringing was a game of risk. Pick up and it could be a cold call pitching you new windows; or a dull peripheral family member; or a loquacious acquaintance. This trepidation remains somewhat, in that I won't answer a call from a number I don't recognise, and there are still calls that, quite frankly, should be a text or an email.

But I have slowly broken away from the grip of the fired-off emoji, or at least lessened its dominance, and started to appreciate an old-fashioned natter. There is a special pleasure to the volley of text banter; but talking to friends or lovers while I lounge on the sofa, or, more often, walk somewhere, has opened up subjects that we've often stopped allocating enough time to (family issues, health concerns, career woes), because they don't fit easily into the communication mediums we have come to rely upon. Meeting up face-to-face isn't always possible, given our increasingly frenetic lifestyles. Or rather, they were frenetic, pre-pandemic; now what's stopping us meeting up face-to-face is lockdown after lockdown. Voicenotes are more likely to be quick thoughts shot off or rambling, solipsistic chains of thought.

It is hard to gauge a proper response from someone after asking them, truly, how they are, if you can't hear the extra intel present in their voice. Typing 'hahaha' will never feel as good as hearing a friend bark with laughter down your ear. A question mark can't fully replace a vocal inflection, can it? I always feel better after speaking on the phone to a pal; it's a shot in the arm during a tiring day. Or sleepily exchanging goodnights, before my head hits the pillow, or just as a pick-me-up when feeling a tad low. What I'm saying is, make like Debbie Harry, and call me.

READING ON
THE BEACH

I am writing this from a beach in Cuba. My fringe has been slicked back by the sea. One half of my face is already the colour of cheap rosé. I am lying under a palm tree to save the other half from a similar fate. And I am reading.

Reading is glorious on any holiday. Reading is glorious full stop. But reading on a beach is something special – though I can't speak for those who live on beaches, or close to them, as to whether or not this is a pleasure dulled by familiarity. (Once you've lived in Oxford for years, you sometimes don't see the magnificent limestone building, just the Pizza Express within.)

But few of us live on a beach like the one I am on. Where the sand is just about as pale as my usual skin colour and the water is so clear it could keep no secrets. Here, to crack open a fresh book, airport-bought, is to mingle the smell of salted skin and the glue binding of a bestseller. In this case, also a Man Booker winner.

There's something about this olfactory combination that gets me every time. I might not experience it for a while, but, when I do, it's like the old friend you can go months without seeing and yet, reunited, you are instantly comfortable.

Reading on a beach pushes a novel to its personal best. Sometimes I think it's the juxtaposition that flexes the imagination. Right now, I am in Cuba, sure, but I'm also – when my pink nose is in between the covers – in 1970s Northern Ireland. One place I'm not? My house, and don't I know it. It's harder here for real life to intrude on my reading focus.

Being a nerd, I also like to take non-fiction books themed around wherever I am going. But it's the fiction that the beach location elevates. Yesterday, my head was so far into a different decade that I hadn't noticed the sun slide across so much sky. I couldn't even hear the clashing sounds of beach sound systems – one of which, unfathomably, is always, everywhere, playing 'Macarena'.

When you finish the first book, the bliss of being on holiday is that you start another right away. Time is presented to you, just the same as a mint on a pillow. When you are home, you will know these books and the trip they took by the sand in their spines and the smudged typeface and the still-sticky pages. You will say, possibly years from now: Ah, yes. *Milkman*. That was an amazing book. I read it in Cuba.

PATTERN

I would find it difficult to muddle through life without pattern; not in the sense of routine, but actual beautiful, artistic patterns. Once, aged eighteen and roaming around Moscow, I spotted an older man wearing an almost exact replica of the blue argyle sweater I had on. I bounded over and suggested a photograph together, and it is now one of my favourites: these two strangers beaming. Neither of us speaking the other's language, but also 100 per cent conversing sartorially. I think of him sometimes and look at that photograph as though it is one of an old friend.

I went through a strong Pringle phase (and suffered many golfing jokes). Then there was a tie-dye era, but that was probably because I was living too close to London's Camden Market at the time. I'm obsessed with damask wallpaper, but too poor to buy Osborne & Little, so I order samples and create collages in the hallway.

A girlfriend gave me a beautiful Persian rug which, as *The Big Lebowski*'s The Dude would have it, really ties the room together. I marvel at it daily. There is a blog dedicated to one man's quest to document every single one of Wetherspoon's carpets (there are 950), which are differently and interestingly patterned, and created on old-fashioned looms.

I love design classics: the Memphis Geometric pattern dominated the 1980s (see Mr Motivator's leotards). Think brightly coloured, random squiggles and triangles, dizzy with the fun of it all; the Pride flag, even if Hannah Gadsby did describe it brilliantly as: 'A bit busy. No rest for the eye.' (The original flag was designed in 1978 by San Francisco artist Gilbert Baker and the colours were coded. Hot pink – not in the current version – was for sex; yellow for sun.) There are the patterns nature gifts us. The glittering, shimmering sun on the surface of the lido. The insane plumage of a Mandarin duck. And, my god, what did we do to deserve giraffes, leopards and tigers?

As a kid, I was transfixed by Magic Eye picture books, kaleidoscopes and making marbled paintings. As an adult, it's the rose windows of cathedrals and the work of Matisse. I'm not Scottish and have no blood ties to France, but is a life lived without tartan and Breton stripes really a life at all?

A FIT OF THE
GIGGLES

We get the giggles. We do not choose the giggles. The giggles choose us. It is entirely the giggles' decision as to when they will join us, and when they will leave us. There is a reason, when I am roaring with laughter, that I say: 'I've lost it.' (If I can get the words out.) There is a reason we refer to them as 'fits' of giggles. It does not matter the place, the time, the inconvenience – we are at their mercy. Our cheeks aching, shoulders shaking, tears streaming, nostrils bubbling.

The giggles are a distillation of pure, exuberant, atavistic happiness. Some episodes are fleeting and do not linger in the memory. Others, when recalling the catalyst, will induce the same reaction for years, perhaps a lifetime. Muscle memory; the particular muscles being those either side of one's mouth.

Laughing is a form of social bonding. (We are 30 per cent more likely to laugh with other people than alone.) It is also contagious. It's possible that I won't find something funny, but the very act of someone else's mirth will set me off.

Giggles do not discriminate. As much as I love them, they have frequently got me into trouble, or caused deep discomfort. Sometimes inappropriateness only serves to exacerbate them. I broke out at my father's funeral when my sister and I were struggling to get out of the car. Of course, the all-over-body laughter made me weaker and I then struggled even more with the door handle. Eventually we tumbled out, creasing up.

I'm not sure I could count on one hand the number of times I have had to excuse myself from the *Guardian*'s daily newsroom conference because something has tickled me so much and won't stop. It is especially difficult to compose myself when catching the eye of the colleague (or colleagues) who caused the laugh attack.

The only time I can remember when the giggles were a heart-stoppingly awful experience – it brings me terror just thinking about it – was when I was on stage at the Southbank Centre. Something, which I will not share here, triggered me in front of 1,000 people, and I spent the next five minutes sweating, squirming furiously and rubbing my palm across my face in a desperate bid to calm myself down, while praying I would not be called upon to say anything. But now, in the comfort of my own home, I am thinking about what set me off. And I have lost it all over again.

BRUSHING TEETH

A few years ago, after coming out of a secure psychiatric ward, I stayed for a couple of weeks in a crisis house. The crisis house is the steppingstone to being fully integrated back into society and one's regular life, which for me basically means drinking a borderline obscene amount of Diet Coke and sending dozens of inappropriate gifs in the middle of the working day.

My room may have been small but the bathroom was huge, and this made me feel safe. I have no idea why. The bars on the window probably helped. Recovering from a detonation of one's brain – I'm not sure that's the technical term – is a lot to do with routine: I was given sleeping pills, and my usual meds were administered at regular times. 'Self-care' took priority. Part of this was my pre-bedtime rituals, which switched from one-too-many cognacs and verbose texts to what I can only describe as an ascetic teeth-brushing regimen.

Of course, before this I wasn't brushing my snappers using a twig and the ashes of oxen's hooves (truly, modernity has blessed us), but I also wasn't spending the fifteen minutes on my teeth that dentists seem to think we have of an evening. Except that suddenly, in that time and place, I did. I would set out my tools on the side of the sink as though a surgeon:

tongue scraper; tongue brush; one of those weird double-ended picks; a frankly disgustingly expensive electronic toothbrush; a strange dye that shows up plaque; two different types of toothpaste (because why not?); floss and those inter-dental brushes (because why choose?).

Sure, you might say this was an attempt to introduce some control into my life, but every single night I had that feeling we all know from leaving the dentist after having our teeth professionally cleaned: when you feel as though your teeth could also produce that cartoon glint in the adverts; when you run your tongue across your central incisors and they feel as though they are made of silk.

These tiny grooming actions we perform can somehow make a big difference when we feel crap. Taking a long shower, slapping on face cream – I'm not saying that having the teeth of Liverpool's Roberto Firmino is going to fix all your problems in life, but it does feel good. It does, somehow, make a glass of water taste purer. It does – look, I don't make the rules – fill one with a sense of a wholesome resetting.

FINDING LOST
THINGS

Grief, if I had to describe the root, is the absence of something. Obviously, there are the serious, life-changing losses: the deaths of family members or friends or pets; redundancy; relationship breakups; when Phoebe Waller-Bridge confirmed there would be only two series of *Fleabag*. But there are also losses with less of an impact and *are* just more annoying, inconvenient, troubling. And here I ask: how glorious is it to find something?

It's the feeling of relief when scrambling around the house for keys and feeling the cold lump of metal under a letter or getting the call that a debit card has been handed in to reception. It's the sensation of luck when the folder of treasured photographs is recovered from an exploded computer. It's the bonus of spotting at the back of the wardrobe an item of clothing you had misplaced months ago. The reward poster that yields results. The passport in a neglected drawer the night before an international flight; panic averted.

I love, too, the delight of getting one's hands on something long sought: an out-of-print book. A perfect G-Plan side table for a bargain price, found in a rural antiques shop, when hours of online browsing turned up nothing. Arriving at a destination, shattered, after hours of driving with an unreliable satnav.

Then there is finding as discovery – stumbling across something you didn't know you were seeking; a wander around town leads to a beautiful statue in a beautiful square. On a larger scale, people talk of finding love, or God; even finding themselves (usually on a Thai island). But I also mean along the lines of finding out a crumbling shopfront in London is, in fact, a toy museum, open according to the owner's whims (I've never been told more times in the space of a few minutes that nothing is for sale).

The truth is, I do not deal well with losing things. Probably because loss is a form of change and I do not deal well with change. Unless it's a change I approve of, such as when Kristen Stewart started dating women. Finding something, though, isn't always enjoyable. When reordering my bookshelves, a slip of paper dropped out of an inside cover: a love note from an ex. Sometimes finding is remembering. And sometimes that is painful or poignant, and one does not want to remember. Reminders are not always good for the mind.

Yet I have the high of a marathon runner when, with the obvious impediment, I manage to find my glasses. I will kiss you on the mouth if you spot the one free table in the pub garden. I will be smug when fingering what I think is a receipt in my pocket and then discover is a £10 note. I will be changing where I keep my passport, though. Some things you don't want to have to find.

BEING WRONG

This might sound strange, and disingenuous, but there is an unexpected pleasure in being wrong. (Of course, this is a rare pleasure for me.) Specifically, the exact moment of realisation. There is also a pleasure in an energetic back-and-forth with a mate, when both of you are convinced that you are correct – but, unless there is some misunderstanding in communication, you cannot both be right. This phase of the argument is also quite eerie because it suggests that you are living in parallel universes. Or that one of you is incredibly drunk.

Depending on the beef, phones will be whipped out; Google fired up; other pals dragged in to take a side. Sometimes it's just a question of whether a word is valid in Scrabble. Sometimes it's a specific thing that did (or did not) happen on a historic night out, or the title of a long-ago film.

I very rarely enter into genuine rifts. Give me a petty difference of opinion or a dispute over a particular fact, however, and I am all over it. At some stage, it may be decided that there is no point continuing the discourse and that age-old phrase will come into play: 'We'll have to agree to disagree'. Which, of course, just means you will no longer discuss the issue, but will internally continue to know absolutely that you are correct. There are two other outcomes: one of you relents and lets the other have their way, despite not being convinced; or one of you genuinely concedes the point.

Of course, it's a total smug joy if your friend, office nemesis or sibling backs down and admits that they are wrong. But, surprisingly, I also find a subtle, sheepish buzz when the penny drops that it is me who is wrong.

I can't fully explain this, other than as a gentle gift of humility, a slice of humble pie that doesn't taste half as bad as you might think and reminds you not to be so stubborn next time. There's also the fact that overcoming disagreements can strengthen bonds. You may even learn something. Bear in mind, though, that it is only enjoyable if the debate was relatively minor and good-natured. There is zero joy in being wrong about something huge. Something friendship-destroying. Something career-ending.

What I am saying is: Lucy, I admit it. You won at bowling in Year 10. I can offer you only a drink and my profuse apologies. I will, however, beat you next time.

BEING RIGHT

Ah, but being *right*. Now isn't that something? The afore-mentioned smug satisfaction, the feigned magnanimity (or perhaps actual magnanimity, if you are a better person than I am). The feeling of providing the correct answer in a pub quiz – when all queried your mighty intellect! – especially if your correct answer contributes to an overall win. It's a pleasure which does not lend itself, I admit, to humility.

This is why people who are *always* right are annoying. More annoying, though, are those who think they are always right, even if they aren't. Being right at the expense of these folk is an even greater delight than just being right in general.

Sometimes being right is down to luck – a casino bet that pays out, for instance. You don't have any direct control over it (although feel free to go on about your superior intuition). Sometimes it's a sense of moral superiority; in the sense of right from wrong. Sometimes, as in the pub quiz, it's smarts. Other times it is more general talent – making the right call as a journalist, picking out the right pass on a sports pitch.

Being wrong in those instances is not the fun type of wrong parsed from banter with a friend. Knowing you have done something ethically wrong feels, for most of us, bad. Doing The Right Thing, however – handing a wallet in, being there for a friend – feels good. Likewise praise from your boss because you have excelled at your job.

These are times when being right gives one a spring in one's step, puts a smile on one's face, and perhaps helps you feel sheepishly proud.

You don't want to be right all of the time, though, because then you wouldn't appreciate it – and you wouldn't appreciate those very specific elements of being wrong that can also amuse. Plus, you would never learn anything and that would just be awful. No, no; that wouldn't be right at all.

RED LIPSTICK

You can spot a baller woman by the fact that she wears no makeup, not a slick of it, except for one thing: a bold red lip. A lot of power women do this and, as with fashion designers who – maybe unexpectedly – seem to wear only black basics (roll-neck sweaters, trainers), it displays a simple self-assuredness. These are women who Get Things Done.

I am one of the women who often goes makeup-free aside from a red lipstick. In my case it is more down to laziness, losing eyeliners and mascara and being exceptionally time poor. I can state with more certainty than Einstein's theory of relativity that I am not in the power-women clan. The thing about a red lip, however, is that – precisely because it is the look of those who have their shit together – it instantly elevates the rest of us. It also signals that you have made an effort, even though that effort has probably taken under a minute.

Everyone suits red lipstick, whereas other shades can wash out complexions, or even terrify; think Fairuza Balk's purple slash of a mouth in *The Craft* or when people attempt quirky orange. Crimson colouring also used to signal a plump, sexualised mouth; Marilyn Monroe, for example. Red was the mark of the femme fatale. The sexy cherry tone of Sherilyn

Fenn as Audrey Horne in *Twin Peaks* (and the seductive tying of an actual cherry knot with her tongue). Rihanna's scarlet pout as she leaves the club, wine glass still in hand.

But now the red lip can be a little more utilitarian. Refreshingly, it is also something that draws the attention and complements facial structure. It is not designed, as with concealer or foundation, to hide. It is the lipstick equivalent of heading the boardroom meeting or walking into the party, shoulders back, chest out. It is also an affordable, accessible slice of glamour.

Sumerians are credited as the inventors of lipstick, followed by super-fans the Egyptians; both women and men would stain their lips with ochre or carmine. Elizabeth I, however, is probably the best known of the scarlet-mouthed. My favourite red lipstick tale, which unfortunately is disputed by historians, is that a law was passed in the 1770s banning it, aligning it with 'witchcraft' and 'trickery'. Disappointing that this probably isn't true, but the fact it's been believed for so long is proof of the red lip's mighty power.

PETTINESS

I am a huge fan of parochial wars over loud flute-playing dominating local newspapers, and adore a pointless petition. Generally, the more extreme the pettiness the greater the delight I take. I feel sick whenever I consider Saudi Arabia's regime, but when the Saudis threatened to dig a canal and turn their nemesis nation Qatar into an island, I could only gasp in admiration at the level of pettiness.

Politics lends itself brilliantly to pettiness. After being sacked as education secretary by Theresa May in 2016, Nicky Morgan responded with a barb about May wearing a pair of £995 leather trousers for a photoshoot. Morgan was then dis-invited from a meeting at Downing Street.

The pettiest person in the world is Donald Trump. It is the only thing to recommend him. The nicknames he gives to his adversaries are wonderful examples of the genre. Perhaps the standout was when he started calling Kim Jong-un 'little rocket man'.

Brexit, meanwhile, is foreign policy via the medium of petty. Nigel Farage deploys similar tactics to Trump. But the Remainer camp projecting messages on to the white cliffs of Dover every time anything went wrong during negotiations (i.e. always, as predicted) is pettiness writ large.

Celebrities, whose lot is essentially to be bullied in the public sphere, take their revenge in small triumphant acts of vengeance: wearing pointed slogan tees or turning the tables by taking photographs of paparazzi photographing them. Breakups are also rich sources of pettiness. See Calvin Harris refusing permission for his ex-girlfriend Rita Ora to perform a song that she recorded, but that he had written.

The best acts of pettiness are knowing. That's what stops them being pathetic. Often there's no benefit to the architect of the pettiness, other than a small satisfaction. The joy of it is that it speaks to the fact that, deep down, we're all just toddlers pretending to be adults.

I leave you with the most majestic act of pettiness ever committed. When E. E. Cummings' first poetry collection was rejected by fourteen publishers, he self-published it with an amended title: *No Thanks*. On the dedication page he wrote a poem entitled 'No Thanks To' and listed each of those publishers who had turned him down. The poem was arranged in the shape of an urn. Just gorgeous.

SECONDHAND
BOOKS

Something I will always, always remember because, even at age fifteen or so, it brought me such joy, was when I bought on eBay a first edition of Sylvia Plath's *Crossing the Water* collection (of course I did) and stuck to the page of the poem 'A Life' was a squished dead fly.

I own a lot of books. Whenever I look for a new place to live, there must be a surfeit of shelving or the space to create it. The books come to me in various ways: as gifts, as new hardbacks from independent bookshops, as last-minute airport paperbacks, sent to the office by publishers (thank you), Amazon deals. My favourites are secondhand editions.

'A life' is a good way to describe it; books have lives. No two people read a book in the same way – each of us brings our experience to bear on a text. The exciting thing about a secondhand book is that one knows at least one other person has done precisely that. While we might not have insight into how exactly that played out, we do have a glimpse into the book's journey. So many clues, each book a sort of Sherlock Holmes case to crack. A handwritten message to a lover on the title page (what ensued?). The notes of a GCSE student getting to grips with their set text (did they pass? Their bored jottings suggest not). Postcards as bookmarks that flutter out from two-thirds in (was the book ever finished?).

The pages yellowed by sunlight. The glorious, musty smell of old classics. A price given in shillings. Pages stuck together from sweaty hands. Crinkled pages from a spilt glass of water or a damp loft. Sand in the centrefold of a trashy beach-holiday read. The jacket of a beautifully designed Penguin Modern Classic clinging on by a sliver of glue. Or detached pages, taped back in.

I love the smell of new books, too, fresh from the printers. But it's the same difference as buying a brand-new top and a vintage dress: you know nobody has gone out and danced the night away in your H&M t-shirt. Nobody has laid their hands upon it, around their partner's waist.

With secondhand things, you might pick up a book that changed a person's life. And that book might change your life. Maybe you will leave it somewhere accidentally, and it will transform someone else's life. Or perhaps they will hate it.

That's the thing about getting a secondhand book: you get two stories in one.

COMPLIMENTS

When I was about twelve, I distinctly remember being in a branch of Sayers the bakers. (Sayers was a popular chain in the north-west before Greggs came along – in completely the same colour scheme, I might add – and somehow became 'cool'. I don't think this injustice has ever been fully acknowledged.)

Anyway, I was in Sayers the bakers and I complimented a woman on her earrings. The woman didn't thank me; she instead looked very embarrassed and proceeded to deliver a five-minute monologue about how rubbish her earrings were. How they were actually really cheap. And the colour washed her out. They weren't real silver, either. These earrings were basically the source of all that was bad in the world.

I remember it because a week before I had read in some teen magazine that girls and women rarely accept compliments – and here was empirical proof. I resolved then to always accept a compliment. In truth, I often add a self-deprecating aside, but, more than I used to, I will just smile and say thank you. It feels good.

Is it better to give or receive? With compliments, as with sex, these are equally pleasurable. I give a lot of compliments. I love to give compliments. I compliment people on the street, sometimes weaving between commuters like the opening scene of a Bond film where he's giving chase, to ask someone where they got their awesome top (it's never, say, 'Jigsaw last month'. Always: 'Oh! A tiny off-the-beaten-track stall in Peru four years ago!').

Most of the time, people beam at random compliments. If someone is looking great, why not tell them? Likewise, if someone has produced something you have really enjoyed, tell them. As a novelist friend once tweeted: 'If you spot a harried husk of an author looking broken in the tinned mysteries aisle at Lidl, and you are considering engaging them in excited chat about their last book . . . do. Made my week.'

We don't often get things for free in this world. But a compliment is free and easy. It can make a heavy heart lift. Or quell an insecurity, or remind you what a good friend somebody is, or that there are benevolent people in the world, just floating about.

I am writing this on the decking of a café, pavement-side. A man just walked past looking very dapper. I told him so. 'Thank you very much!' he replied. I can see him walking into the distance, grinning.

SATURDAY'S
PAPERS

When it comes to Saturday papers, to paraphrase Brian Clough, I'm not saying the *Guardian* is the best, but it's definitely in the top one.

Amid lowering circulations, Saturday remains the most popular day of the week for readers to pop to the shops and get ink all over their hands during breakfast. (We increasingly bury our heads on social media or apps to get our fix during the week.) Despite the fact that much of the UK press is on the verge of becoming stenography, I still enjoy reading a broad spectrum, spreading the different titles and supplements across the table, like William S. Burroughs and his cut-up collages. The *Telegraph* has great arts pages; the *FT*'s weekend edition is a fat joy; *The Times* has interesting features.

The weekends, our break from scrolling through the week's quagmire, are meant for folding back pages, for supplements sliding out of centrefolds, and failing at sudokus. If it is a sunny day, and you are reading outside, the heat makes the paper give off an earthy, relaxing scent. Reading the papers is about sitting under trees, the simultaneous rustle of leaves and pages. Or baked-bean juice spilling from a greasy-spoon plate on to the margins. Or the celebrity interview earned after a run and a shower.

On Saturday, I will read all about sports that I don't understand the point of (or the point systems of). I will dive into travel supplements even if I cannot afford to go away – and especially not to places where penguins are found on beaches. Because it is the act of reading itself that is the pleasure of Saturday papers – not the urgent need for news to be imparted.

It is taking the time to run the eye over photo essays and to read a startling review of a book that may turn out to be more fulfilling than the book itself. If not your life, then I'm talking about measuring out your day in coffee spoons – and colour profiles. Sometimes it's the cheeky high of nicking a battered copy from the pub and reading it on the way home.

I even like to get the international papers: the *New York Times*, the *Washington Post*. Queen-bed-sized broadsheets that block out the morning light when held open, allowing your partner to snooze a little longer. Print's demise is much discussed; it's an industry on the edge. But I can't imagine Saturdays that don't leave the recycling bin bulging. And neither, I'd guess, can you.

BEING A REGULAR

There are the obvious people in our lives with whom we spend lots of time: a spouse, children, extended family, friends, colleagues. Those you would expect. But isn't it true that we often see far more frequently the cashier at the local shop; the waitress at the nearby cafe; the lifeguard at the pool?

This is the joy of being a regular. I create bonds significant enough with those I interact with on a daily basis that last year, when going to my usual breakfast place first thing on the morning of my birthday, the staff all came out singing, with a candle in a piece of toast. And the only thing that would get me through the days when I was deeply depressed was the conversations with – and free bananas from – the guy who worked in the corner shop, Zain. I would tell myself that if I got out of bed and walked to the end of the street and spoke to Zain, that was something.

Zain sensed the darkness that descended, but he never addressed it directly, just looked up from the cricket on his iPhone and high-fived me – and kept me in potassium.

I don't live in that neighbourhood any more. Now I have a new corner shop. A different gym, a different station, a different cinema. I am a new regular. There is the pharmacist who looks out for me – a team of three, in fact – because they know

I am extremely skilled at leaving my prescription to the last minute. There is the restaurant that brings my order without me asking (silent communication is the apex of all communication; the first time in a relationship you both watch the TV without feeling the need for a running commentary, for example). There are the receptionists in the office who seem to know before I do when I have forgotten my pass.

This is the joy of people, the joy of place – and the combination of the two. Because being a regular is lots of things: belonging somewhere, being accepted, understood. Being acknowledged, even. Being a regular is what can stave off the loneliness for older people without family, or the freelancer eking out a coffee for eight hours.

The places themselves soothe, too. The familiarity of the wifi name or the exact sensation of upholstery on the back of the thigh, in the chair that is your chair, in your corner.

I am a regular. I have my places. And when I move, I carry them with me.

CLOSING
BROWSER TABS

When I was a kid, *The World's Strongest Man* was televised each year during the fallow period between Christmas Day and New Year. The thing I remember most was the sheer release on the faces of men built like tree trunks when they stopped pulling a train, or rearranging Atlas Stones that had made ribbons of their forearms.

That's the relief I feel when clearing all my internet browser's tabs. Clicking the crosses like a long line of kisses finally indulged. There are many reasons why one has tabs open in double figures. In my defence, they are often related to work or research. The sense of lightness that comes over me when closing them is down to a task completed. It is a bit like setting one's pen down at the end of an exam; the way the air feels that bit fresher coming out of the hall than going in.

Then there are the cajoling tabs bursting with opportunities to procrastinate. The icons of social media accounts winking alluringly or the random YouTube clip pulled up and watched four times for no apparent reason. I cannot tell you the number of tabs I have open on 10,000-word long reads that I will eventually, ostensibly, 'get round to'. Closing these unread would be to acknowledge defeat, and so they just stay there, like a guest at a party whom you would like to leave but are too anxious to throw out.

When I first moved to the offices of the *Guardian*, I was quite shocked to find each individual had but a single monitor. Where I had previously worked, each of us had a two-monitor setup that meant our tabs could be spread across two wide screens. I see now that this only encouraged the habit. Because tabs, like gases, expand to fill their container. I will even open new windows to accommodate more of them. Sometimes I have more than one browser open and my desktop ends up looking like a game of solitaire.

We should take the same approach with tabs as when sorting a closet or bookshelf: if a tab has been dormant for a certain length of time, it should go. It's only a moment's work and doesn't involve the crushing revelation that 90 per cent of your cashmere has been eaten by moths and everything else left untouched.

Close your tabs. All of them. One fell swoop. No looking back. If you need something, you will already have it bookmarked, or you will remember it well enough to revisit. Un-tab yourself. It's pretty much the only life advice I am qualified to give.

CHEATING A
HANGOVER

Brace yourself. That is the first thing that enters one's head after a heavy night out, before the eyes are even open. Sometimes, listing nausea or a banging in the brain is what wakes us in the first place. We all know that if someone invented a cure for hangovers – and boy, have they tried – that person would be very rich indeed and worshipped as a deity.

It doesn't matter if it has been one too many after work drinks or cracking open a second bottle of wine with one's partner: the consequences of over-indulgence patiently lie in wait.

It's the knowledge that a brutal hangover reduces one to a quivering husk – a sweaty bundle of anxiety, a half-person with memories as fuzzy as static – that underlines one of the greatest escapes any of us can enjoy: the Houdini-level trick that is Waking Up Without A Hangover.

I know two types of non-hangover intimately. The first became my normal when I was sober for a year, and it was glorious. Clocks seemed to expand with time. I was – and I'm afraid there's no other word for it – sprightly. But waking up without a hangover after a night of getting plastered, when, by rights, one's liver should spend all day in the foetal position, is one of life's true gems. It's the world saying: here, have one on me.

74

A warning though: pride comes before a fall. Many of us know the false sense of security, an assertion that 'Oh, I feel fine'. Cut to the afternoon and a delayed hangover has worked its way into one's insides like bindweed. It's a bit like chatting to a stranger at a pub, having a jolly good time, then boom – racist comment. You didn't see it coming and it's all the worse for that.

The genuine hangover-free day, though? Truly a chef's kiss. Of course, life being as it is, it's a treat overwhelmingly likely to occur on a languid Saturday, when vomiting into one's loo wouldn't be the end of the world. The devilish hangovers, meanwhile, the ones that feel like a raw deal after what one thought was actually 'a pretty chilled night', will, inevitably, happen on the Wednesday morning of an important work presentation.

I am sure scientists could tell us the reasons for discrepancies: the type of beverage imbibed; or mixing drinks; amounts of food eaten; water consumed. But to me it always feels like Russian roulette, an absence of rhyme or reason. We play the booze game and we take our chances. And it's immensely satisfying when we win.

ACKNOWLEDGE-
MENTS

I have something to acknowledge: I love acknowledgements. They are the first thing I read in a book. (Often I won't read an author's introduction until after I have finished, in case it contains spoilers.)

Gratitude is one of the most important things. If someone doesn't say thank you after I hold a door open for them, they might as well be a serial killer. Acknowledgements are the literary equivalent of thanking all the people who made a book possible; who held the door open. (Or gave the writer a key to their cottage by the sea for a writing retreat. Lots of those.)

I am quite a nosy person, so I enjoy scanning the names to see if there is someone I recognise; it is as though I have spotted two people I did not know were friends dining together in a restaurant. I enjoy the turns of phrase writers come up with to avoid repeating themselves. The in-jokes.

We even get a glimpse into the circumstances of an author's life and the backdrop against which the book was produced. Those who acknowledge Arts Council grants or thank the NHS, and even food banks and housing charities, as was the case in Anna Burns's Booker-winning novel *Milkman*; a mini political commentary in itself.

I am currently reading Benjamin Dreyer's brilliant *Dreyer's English*, which has eight pages of acknowledgements; a commendable level of generosity (though if this were an Oscars speech, the orchestra would have played him off by the second page). I suppose the longer the list, the more likely someone will be miffed if left out; but also, the shorter the list, the danger that more people will be miffed. What a minefield.

Dedications are much more likely to be read, being right at the start of the book, so funny or touching ones are often more memorable than something similar tucked away at the back. What a shame, though, if the acknowledgements page at the back of Brendan Pietsch's *Dispensational Modernism*, which starts: 'I blame all of you', had gone unnoticed.

But it's the love coming off the pages that make acknowledgements so special. Knowing that the book I am about to read (for others, usually the book just read) could not have come into being without all the support and advice and friendship and hard work of others. The reiteration that, no matter the trope of the toiling writer in a solitary study, life – in all its glory and achievement – is a team sport.

COLD-WATER
SWIMMING

I wouldn't say it was extremely comforting when, seconds before my first attempt at cold-water swimming at my local pond, as I hovered near the steps, my skin chill against the air, the jovial lifeguard started to tell me about sudden-immersion syndrome. 'People can die, because they go into shock,' she explained, eyes focused on something in the distant trees. 'But you'll be fine. Just don't panic.'

In the summer, I jump into the pond with the enthusiasm of a labrador – ears flying, paws spread skywards. (This was especially the case during last summer's heatwave, two months of feeling conflicted – the utter joy of that slightly grassy smell of warm forearms, tempered by the fact that the planet is, well, screwed.) Summer swimming is all about the refreshing feel of hair slicked back from the forehead after hours of enduring a sticky, matted mess. Or the tessellating, shimmering patterns of light at the bottom of a hotel pool.

Cold-water swimming is like being plugged into the mains; there is the sensation of a sedentary life spent looking at screens cracking wide open. It's a body slam-dunking in every department: heart, lungs, brain. The first time, I thought of Jack and Rose in *Titanic*, as she considers jumping overboard and he tries to talk her out of it: the water will 'hit you like a thousand knives stabbing you all over your body'. (Incidentally, has there been a more handsome man than Leonardo DiCaprio in *Titanic*? This is a rhetorical question.)

Jack isn't wrong, but knives have their uses. Knives can cut binds and set people free. At times I feel so bad that there is a restless ennui, a nihilistic velocity – every human atom bares its teeth; the shock of the cold water takes the edge off that inner violence. There has even been recent research that cold-water swimming can help with depression and anxiety, by improving the stress response.

I'm no expert swimmer. I wear the same thing in all temperatures – a humble bikini. It's from Topshop – or somewhere similar that might pay its taxes and isn't owned by Philip Green. There are stronger swimmers who go more often than I do, kitted out in wetsuits and special waterproof thermal gloves and hats.

But even when it's deep winter in the city and I look as if I took a wrong turn on the way to the Costa del Sol, I feel a sense of pride when I've met the challenge of 5°C scrawled on the chalkboard, as satisfying as a maths equation solved. 'Reinvigorating' is an overused word in an era of self-help books and journeys to faraway continents to find oneself, but cold-water swimming is truly that.

BLUE PLAQUES

Peter Kropotkin was a prince and a theorist of anarchism. The incongruously named Charles Coward rescued prisoners from Auschwitz. Edvard Beneš was a president of Czechoslovakia. What do these people have in common? Their names are on a royal-blue ceramic, metal or plastic circle.

The original blue plaque scheme was established by the Royal Society of Arts (then just the Society of Arts) in 1866 to mark the relationships between certain buildings and individuals. The first was placed on Lord Byron's birthplace in Cavendish Square, in London, although that house has since been demolished.

Since 1986, the scheme, which is exclusive to the capital, has been run by English Heritage. Blue plaques have become so well known that they deserve their own blue plaque. But other bodies administer them around the UK. There are now green, yellow, brown, black and red plaques, as well as white, pink and rainbow plaques. The colours vary according to geography or theme: red for transport heritage; rainbow for LGBTQ+ champions. There are plaques, too, in other parts of the world. It is even possible to buy one's own novelty plaque.

I will never tire of a blue plaque. I cannot count the number of times I have walked by one, then caught it out of the corner of my eye and doubled back to learn that an eminent physicist once rented a room in such-and-such Georgian home, or that an author died at a tragically young age in this Victorian terrace. Some plaques commemorate movements, moments, events, records or institutions rather than people. Every time I read one, it is as though the street has opened like a textbook.

There are two main reasons for my appreciation. The first is a nerdy passion for facts. The second is the beautiful way the plaques evoke a place as it once was: Bloomsbury Square, say, as Virginia Woolf would have known its corners. I love the idea that one might bend down to do up a lace on the exact spot that a rock star stopped to light a cigarette. Then there are the plaques attached to the houses you can barge right into: John Lennon's in Liverpool, or Sigmund Freud's in north London.

But it is the quirkier ones that really lift the spirits. Tommyfield in Oldham has a plaque that announces it as the home of fried chips. A plaque in Tottenham, London, is dedicated to Luke Howard, 'namer of clouds'. The greatest, though, might be on a council block in Brighton, erected by the Centre for Pagan Studies: Doreen Valiente, the 'mother of modern witchcraft', we salute you.

LITTLE ACTS OF KINDNESS

A little while ago, I was sitting on a bench, reading, when an elderly lady approached me. 'Excuse me,' she asked. 'Would you be able to help me with my shopping?'

I beamed. Of course I would be able to help her with her shopping! Let's get this shopping-helping show on the road, I wanted to shout. For I am an excellent person and enthusiastic assistant to those in need. Unfortunately, it turned out she didn't mean shopping as a metonym for shopping bags, but as in . . . the verb. She had not yet been to the shop. This was not me lifting two Lidl bags and carrying them to the bus stop, as I had envisaged; this was me going to Lidl.

Forty-five minutes later, this wily elder of mine – who had also swindled me out of £3 by this point and made a fair few comments I would describe as bigoted – let me know that she lived on the top floor of a block of flats but, not to worry, because the block was only a mile or so away. Despite all this – 'this' being the entire afternoon – I still feel contented that I helped this lady out, even if I have avoided her since.

Good deeds are considered selfless, but they are often not. This is because a fair number of good deeds take minimal effort; the effort is outweighed by the feeling of self-satisfaction. If anything, it is pure human profit, and as such perhaps not altruistic at all. (There are, of course, the times when we go above and beyond, when we inconvenience ourselves for others. I can summon up many occasions when friends, all over the world and in all seasons, have gone above and beyond for me.)

However, mostly it's something that, for you, takes very little, but can make all the difference to another. The teenage girl frantic in a strange city who asks for directions, or to borrow your phone. Lifting someone's suitcases down station stairs or grabbing one end of a frazzled mother's pram, its inhabitant blotchy-faced and screaming. Tapping a rushed businessman on the shoulder to return his wallet.

I truly believe the whole world would collapse without these interactions, or to use the American argot: the act of paying it forward. In fact, one doesn't need to be the do-gooder or the recipient to be warmed by an act of kindness. Even reading about them can be a joy. Do a good deed today, then – even if it's just holding a door open. And I will do one for someone in turn. As long as it's not their entire weekly shop. Never again.

BATHS

As a nipper, although frankly I mean until about the age of eighteen, I wasn't keen on baths. I was hyperactive and staying still for a period of five minutes or longer required effort. As a teenager, I found baths not conducive to my lifestyle, which mostly consisted of being late. Quicker bathing meant more sleep; more texting; more listening to indie bands with unfathomable names made up of punctuation.

Then: a mid-twenties baptism into the devoutness of baths. A love of soaking bubbled to the surface. This love smells of lavender and bergamot oil. It feels like the damp, crinkled edges of book and magazine pages. It sounds like nothing, aside from the quiet swish and gargle of water when rearranging limbs. It tastes of the mug of tea balanced precariously on the side (but not so precariously as to be anxiety-making). I have a friend, Greg, who enjoys nibbling at cheese while in the bath; he even creates a little foil boat for it. He is an icon.

I cannot pinpoint the 'Eureka!' moment (Archimedes' famous bath pronouncement) but it was probably around the time I swapped tagging pictures of nights out on social media for browsing Mumsnet for tips on moth control, AKA sinking into a premature middle age. What do babies and I have in common? We both have a strict 7 p.m. bathtime.

Running a bath is an art. What I Talk About When I Talk About Running a Bath: well, screw up temperature control and the experience can spill into disappointment. Either the water cools too quickly, forcing one out before time (as with getting to the pool too close to the whistle for a decent swim). Or the water is too hot, and one is left sweating profusely and feeling faint; philtrum transforming into an oxbow lake, knees turning a football-club red. But get the perfect temperature, and worries evaporate. Intrusive thoughts are sweated out.

As with purposely taking long bus journeys, I use my time in the tub to read. It is rare that I take my phone into the bathroom, because if I really can't last an hour without it then I might as well let the waves take me. Of course, there is also the small matter of cleaning oneself. A good scrubbing of the back. A leg lolling over the side, being smoothed. A face mask that resembles a muddy accident. Standing up to get out, the tired hours of the day cascade away. Woes circle the drain. We float on.

ARRIVING EARLY

I am a chronically late person. I am not proud of this. It is a flaw in my character and, I am certain many of you reading will agree, a significant one. Some people don't seem to mind tardiness. I am lucky to know quite a few such people. Others understandably find chronic lateness the height of rudeness and emblematic that an individual values their own time over that of everyone else.

My main issue is that I am easily distracted. I am somewhat childlike in my facility to have my attention captured by, well, literally anything. Most people grow out of this, but I seem to have grown further into it. (Although I suppose children don't regularly catch sight of an interesting coverline on a copy of the *New Yorker* lying around the house and get drawn into a 20,000-word article while shower-wet hair begs to be dried.)

A diagnosis of ADHD, long suggested by colleagues, has finally been been confirmed by a psychiatrist. In certain phases of mental ill health, I find it difficult to gear myself up to leave the house and feel deeply that my presence will only ruin any social event. So sometimes there are genuine reasons. Although I feel citing the studies that suggest lateness is associated with intelligence might be going too far. I think, with me, it has something to do with optimism.

It is a contented bliss, then, to be early. Habitual early birds probably will not experience this high. But I have a theory that one of the purest forms of happiness is relief. Relief has a lightness that unlocks carefreeness, which speaks to freedom, and freedom is happiness.

The extreme tension I feel when rushed and late, despite it being self-inflicted and a social form of self-harm, means that when I do manage to be on time, or, even better, early, it's a felicity to savour. As an individual who will sometimes forget keys but never a paperback, any unexpected portion of time for reading is exciting. Earliness also offers the opportunity for observation; seeing the things one misses when flitting between modes of public transport and walking with the determined velocity of Richard Ashcroft in the video for 'Bittersweet Symphony'. Or I'll just think about who I am meeting and how pleasing it will be to spend time with them. Still, it will take a little more time (natch) for earliness to stick.

WALLPAPER

I am not saying I do not live an exciting and fulfilling life, but I enjoy ordering A4 samples of wallpaper online. I am saying that I truly believe the moment capitalism spiralled out of control was when homeware stores started charging for tester pots of paint. I am saying I've bought a plant from Homebase to cover my shame when walking out with rolls and rolls of the test wallpaper one tears off the racks like clingfilm.

All this forms what I am going to refer to as the 'renter's renovation'. Long-term renters will know that only minimal changes to decor are permitted. Renters will also know that a single gossamer strand of cobweb spotted in a moving-out inventory check can see a portion of deposit chalked off.

But, like most of us, I love to put my stamp on a place; to match up my personality to my environment. And I love wallpaper. I square the renter's dilemma by using literal squares; I order lots of sample wallpaper and create a collage on a distinct section of wall.

I affix the wallpaper using glue in the corners and middle, which can be easily and totally cleaned off, rather than proper permanent paste. Though I despise the term 'feature wall', that is essentially what this process produces: a pleasing, DIY display of colour and pattern and design.

Wallpaper, like everything, goes in and out of fashion. When I was growing up, it was definitely out of fashion. Now it has had a renaissance. Queen Anne even introduced a wallpaper tax (in 1712, it lasted until 1836). One way people got round it was to buy plain paper and stencil it. Which I like to think is the sort of creative-thinking antecedent to what I do. I've never actually understood why this tax was introduced, so I assume Anne had some sort of traumatic wallpaper-related incident and held a grudge.

Many styles have flourished throughout history: Baroque designs, hand-painted Chinese landscapes, silk damasks, floral patterns, flock, 1960s Pop Art varieties, the orange-and-brown scrub-down vinyl of the 1970s, abstract. The Arts and Crafts stylings of the King of Wallpaper, William Morris, remain favourites of mine.

At various times, the wallpaper industry has been screwed by such events as the Napoleonic wars and even the 1973 oil crisis, but it goes on surviving, seeing off challenges from awful, cloying wall decals (Live, Laugh, Fuck Off). Not even the discovery that George Osborne is the son of the co-founder of Osborne & Little could quell my passion. Wherever I sort-of-hang my wallpaper, that's my home.

FLIRTING

Calling someone a 'flirt' isn't seen as an insult, but in some cases it might serve as a snide sort of traducing. It's also not great reputationally at the moment, post-#MeToo. But I would argue that those who have responded to #MeToo by moaning that, 'God, nobody is allowed to flirt any more,' might just have flirting very wrong indeed.

Flirting is lovely. I am a flirt. I flirt all the time. There is, for me, both a spoken language of flirting and a bodily one. In conversation, there is something of a frisson to a wonderful, witty back and forth. I might not be physically attracted to my interlocutor – hell, it might even be a friend, and the idea of hooking up weird – but it's the thrill of the exercise. I hesitate to say that language is sexy, but also: it is.

I am a big fan of physical contact. Obviously, one must be attuned to those who are not so keen (and yes, there are times when it is inappropriate, but again, these circumstances should not be difficult to determine). I live for an enveloping hug. An upper-arm squeeze; a casual knee tap; an arm slung around a shoulder; a wide smile; a hair ruffle; lifting a stray eyelash from a cheek; holding hands; linking arms. This behaviour is second nature to me, with friends, with friendly colleagues, with people I meet at parties who

I'm getting on with riotously. Touch is so important.

People frequently see flirting as a prelude to sex. Clearly, the former can very much lead to the latter. But as the above examples show, this is by no means always the case. If I straighten a colleague's tie and dust off his shoulders, it's a form of flirting, but I don't want to shag him. If I'm sitting close to someone, drink in hand, and I gently slap their leg when they make me laugh. Well . . . maybe I want to kiss them, but other times, that wouldn't even occur to me.

These aren't mixed messages. I think I make it pretty obvious whether my flirting is a mechanism to signal sexual interest, or just the way my enjoyment of an interaction manifests itself. And people who know me well, know that I am tactile. The phrase 'harmless flirting' exists for a reason. Plus, at the end of the day – well, any time of the day – who doesn't want to be flirted with?

POT PLANTS

I fully agree that we need to be more proactive about teaching schoolchildren the fundamentals of modern life. Financial education; preparation for the world of work; explanations of how mortgages and rental contracts work . . . lessons like these would mean that come their early twenties young people might not feel so stressed and adrift.

One thing in particular: how did I get to my mid-twenties without knowing that it is possible to murder a plant by overwatering it? Water is the elixir of life. I did not think anything could be bad about water.

The popularity of pot plants has risen in the past decade or so. This is mocked as a hipster affectation rather than being seen for what it truly is – a relatively cheap and easy way for the masses in rental apartments to put their stamp on a place. And to make it feel homely, when tenancies are often insecure and painting the walls can result in losing thousands of pounds in a deposit.

It seems slightly uncouth for elders, sitting on property assets, to mock my generation for enjoying a spider plant in the sitting room, a baby fern in the bathroom, a cactus in the kitchen. Add to this the fact that it is scientifically proven that contact with nature and greenery (any contact – even a view) is beneficial to mental health, and the boom in pot plants is even more understandable. Pot plants have been found to increase people's productivity by up to 15 per cent.

Did I ever think I would become a person who got excited about a weekend trip to a garden centre? Reader, I did not.

I may not have learned the scientific (i.e., Latin) names for most plants, but then I can also listen to albums all the way through and not know the titles of the songs I love. And aren't we supposed to be living in a time of diminishing importance of labels?

As for my plant-caring skills, the turning point came when an ex-partner bought me a bonsai (I named him Yury; I don't know why but he is definitely a he). I have managed to keep Yury going for two years, which was longer than I managed to keep the relationship alive.

THREE-MINUTE
POP SONGS

I used to be a huge fan of Phil Spector. Then he was convicted of murder, which rather took the shine off things. But Spector, I'm afraid, remains for me the king of pop. Spector is the king because his 'wall of sound' production formula gave us the doo-wop gems of the Ronettes and the Crystals and went on to influence surf-pop unbeatables the Beach Boys.

While I'm keen on a dramatic eight-minute epic to close a rock album, a pop song should come in at between two and three minutes (as almost every track on *Pet Sounds* does). That's why, when Madonna brought out a song that was four minutes long called '4 Minutes' she was not as clever as she thought she was. Also, the radio edit was not four minutes. Also, it was crap.

The three-minute pop track is a legacy of the 78rpm of shellac and then vinyl records, a single side of which lasted between three and five minutes. Now, with no such restrictions, tracks can tend to bloviation. Most of the truly great bangers still come in at under three minutes. The raucous teen energy of Arctic Monkeys' debut single 'I Bet You Look Good on the Dancefloor', at 2 min 54 sec, is a perfect example. However, I have come to allow circa 3 min 30 sec as an acceptable length. That is because of Xenomania, the production outfit that worked with Girls Aloud throughout their career. As anybody with taste knows, Girls Aloud were the best pop group in decades. Thanks to Xenomania, they pumped out hit after hit. 'Biology' – which owes much to the doo-wop sound – is essentially three songs in one, all in a neat 3 min 35 sec.

The pleasure of shorter pop songs is the simple prioritising of quality over quantity. A techno masterpiece that has a five-minute intro of glitches and ear-ruining bass is right up my street; but a long running time for a pop song instantly signals dull filler effects or a lot of 'Uh, yeah!' interludes.

Pop songs are mini-stories and should be the audio equivalent of Raymond Carver's finest . There is a reason radio edits last about three minutes: because that is how songs should have been born. Is it a coincidence that Abba's 'Waterloo' and the Kinks' 'You Really Got Me' are both under three minutes? It is not.

If you really want to show off, you could follow Queen's example: 'We Will Rock You' comes in at a stupendously slender 2 min 2 sec. It leaves you wanting more, and that's precisely what the perfect number is supposed to do. Three minutes, repeat ad infinitum.

COMPERSION

The words jealousy and envy are often used interchangeably, but they mean different things. Jealousy is when one is anxious or fearful that someone will take away what one already has – which is why we talk of jealous partners.

Envy is wanting what another has. We say we are 'jealous' when we see someone's holiday pictures on Instagram, but in fact we are envious. It's an antisocial emotion, and one we've all felt.

Some psychologists recognise, however, something known as 'benign envy': rather than stewing and wishing the downfall of those who have things or experiences we covet, we are inspired by their success to work harder and achieve the same.

Then there is something even more benign: feeling *actively* happy about someone else's success, divorced from any self-interest. There's a lot of humour to be mined in a friend squealing to another, 'I'm so happy for you!' but dying inside with a brought-to-the-boil feeling of: why not me?

Feeling genuine joy at another's joy is a thing. It's known as *muditā* in Buddhism. (There's also a German term, *Mitfreude*, which would serve as the opposite to schadenfreude.) The fact that the former is not widely used, but the latter is well-known worldwide probably tells us something. Recently, another term has emerged, in English, for this vicarious pleasure: compersion. Meaning empathic pleasure.

Sometimes compersion is easy. I don't want children, so if a friend announces they are pregnant, then, OK sure, I'm slightly pissed off at the thought of losing another one of my pals to nappies, but it's not difficult for me to be genuinely happy for them. But if one is unsuccessfully trying for a baby, it would be natural to feel envious.

As adults we are meant to be better at handling jealousy and envy. Perhaps that is why I have stood beaming at so many friends' book launches and been thrilled to attend house-warming parties at homes I could never afford. Of course, the temptation is there to lock the new owners in the bathroom and squat in it, but most of all I am happy for them. And, more importantly, I mean it.

VIDEO GAMES

As a kid, I wasn't outside playing football or tennis, I was playing them inside on a PlayStation, or a friend's Nintendo or X-Box. I loved video games. I used to play alone a lot, by which I mean I spent more time with an avatar of pro-skateboarder Tony Hawk than with some of my actual family members, but it was playing with friends that was the most fun.

These days people do not need friends to be in the same room for them to play video games together. Many people play online with strangers across the world. But back in the late 1990s, this, and multi-player platforms, was not a thing. Back in the late 1990s, it was all about jelly shoes, troll dolls . . . and the secondary controller.

Consoles came (and probably still do) with a single controller. Purposely, as it meant that consumers had to buy another. Often this meant that players had one official controller and one generic version that had been bought at half the price. There was definitely a power dynamic to who got the official controller and who got the knock-off. A visiting player knew their status; and that was the user of the unofficial controller. There's basically no difference whatsoever, but it still seems rude.

I distinctly recall the thrill of shuffling into a cross-legged position, setting down a fizzing glass of soda, and waiting for the homescreen of a game to fire up. The arcade sounds bursting into life as characters, teams and settings are swiped across onscreen and choices made. Important choices. Choices to alter the next few hours of your life.

There was no more wholesome high than mashing the buttons of a controller, feeling its vibrations against the palms and wiggling a thumb around a joystick – all while telling your parent over your shoulder, that, no, neither of you or your friend are hungry, but thank you for asking, many, many times.

I grew out of video games, but any time I end up randomly playing them with a friend in their house, that same thrill comes back. I no longer have any talent or understand the tricks and tips that make a player accomplished, but somehow semi-screaming 'no, no, no, no' as the car you are virtually driving skids towards the barriers of the track is exhilarating. Somehow the swagger of a computerised football player during his goal celebration translates to real life and rushes from the screen, down the wires, into your own body.

During the pandemic lockdown, I considered buying a console, but I realised that I wouldn't find it fun enough by myself. That I longed to just muck about as a pal is half-frustrated with me being, really, really bad, and half-elated by knowing they will win. One day soon, we might even be allowed in each other's houses, at which point, I will gladly lose all over again.

AIRPLANE MODE

I remember, because I am petty, an argument I had with an air steward years ago. 'I'm sorry, but you'll have to turn your phone off while we take off,' she said. 'Oh, it's on airplane mode,' I replied. 'Yes, but while we take off, you'll have to turn the device off.' 'But it's on . . . airplane mode,' I said again. 'This is what it's for. This situation. That's even . . . that's the name.' She wasn't having it.

Being British, 'aeroplane mode' would be a more accurate description, but because Silicon Valley has now swallowed the Earth and we're all just addicts being buried alive, the American 'airplane mode' is what most of us call the setting that prevents signal transmission, thereby disabling calls, text messages and wifi. It is the way we switch off – without actually switching off. It allows us a pause in the constant chatter of life. It is a deep breath of the analogue. It's a small toggle that allows the brain the equivalent of kicking one's shoes off when home and sprawling across the sofa.

Of course, having the healthy option on offer doesn't mean we choose it. Quite often, I let the choice of airplane mode drift. I tell myself I won't look at my phone for a little bit, but I don't actually go the full mile and turn on airplane mode. What if there's an urgent message (by which I mean an amusing gif)?

But the rewards when strapping oneself in, tightening the belt and committing, are sublime. Take a walk when airplane mode is on and pull your phone out every now and again to alter music choices, or snap pics, safe from news-app push notifications and missed calls. Safe from the WhatsApp discourse pinballing on to the lockscreen.

Airplane mode needs to fulfil its potential; it should not be confined to cinemas and theatres, concert halls and examination rooms. And, well, airplanes. Airplane mode needs to spread its wings and take us under them. More and more, I feel we need the protection of the natural, or the unplugged. We need to step over cables. Not via a tech-free villa in Ibiza, but with some self-discipline.

Airplane mode is one of the few things that facilitates this. It's better than a distraction, because it shuts the jaws of the thing itself. I don't know whose idea it was, but I'd like to shake their hand and take them for a drink – strictly no phones allowed.

A LAST-MINUTE
GOAL

As a homegrown and lifelong Liverpool supporter, their extraordinary 2019/20 season was nothing short of ecstasy.* I am unfortunate enough to have been born just as our 1980s period of domination ended and so have had to suffer fierce rivals Manchester United lording it over us in the league (and overtaking us in number of league titles won) ever since. But in 2020 Liverpool finished eighteen points clear at the top of the table. The season before that, we lost the league by a single point. We had one Premier League defeat over the entire run: to Manchester City, who then went on to win the title. That game is the perfect example of the incredibly thin margins that matches, in any sport, can hinge on. Liverpool lost 2-1. A deflection off a City player went into the goal – but was judged not to have wholly crossed the line. We didn't just lose the league by one point; we lost it by one centimetre.

It is high-octane situations such as this that make sport so thrilling. The heart leaping at the umpire's call. The sweaty palms waiting to see which colour card a referee will brandish. But my god; nothing beats the last-minute – sometimes the last-second – winning goal. In 2012, City became champions

* Suffice to say, the 2020/21 season I did not find ecstatic.

in not just the last minute of the game, but the last minute of the entire league. The ninety-fourth minute, in fact. The jubilation for those fans!

We love sport because it takes us out of ourselves. It builds communities and forges connections. It entertains. Though it can bring us hot tears of frustration, it can also bring us immense pleasure. A millisecond of time in return for a gigantic triumph, conduited by a twenty-year-old local lad. Or perhaps a kid from the other side of the world, who honed his or her skills in rotting trainers and made it out against all the odds. What could be more soul-lifting?

The joy of a last-minute goal is a similar feeling to sliding on to a train just as the doors are closing. Or running, shoes and lungs pounding, to catch a bus – and making it. Or hitting a deadline with moments to spare. I can't scientifically explain why this is so much more satisfying than achieving something in good time, but maybe it's the excitement of living on the edge. And what could be more exciting than a football rippling the back of the net, when all appears lost?

A CUP OF TEA

I am not sure what I'd do without tea. 70 per cent of the Earth's surface is water; 70 per cent of my body is tea. Hook me up to a hospital drip of the stuff and I doubt I'd notice the difference.

As I write, I have a mug of it at my elbow – we keep close the things we love most. It's an Earl Grey number, my brew of choice. This, despite previously dismissing it as having 'very strong notes of soap'. (I may have been using a bergamot body wash around the same time I first tried it.)

It's not just Earl Grey I enjoy. A classic builder's is a familiar pleasure. Camomile helps me unwind in the evening. Green grew on me. I like to throw in a forest-fruit blend now and again, just to mix it up. Black with lemon I picked up from living in Russia. Sometimes I consider moving to America and three things so far have stopped me: the jaywalking laws, the dismal healthcare system, and the fact that no one there owns an electric kettle.

The best things in life – people, places, ideas or things – are adaptable. That is the thing about tea, too: it's appropriate in many situations. The popular imagination is au fait with tea as a comforter, of course. (How do teachers of English as a second language convey that 'I'll stick the kettle on' contains multitudes?) I've even had a policewoman make me tea in my own home.

There is also debrief tea: a round of mismatched mugs in a friend's sunny garden, a bunch of you having stayed over after a party. There is procrastinatory tea (seven in the space of an hour). There is tea to warm you and, although you wouldn't think it, tea to cool you down. Tea to help you think. Tea to stop you thinking. Then there is tea as a helpful marker of character. You should see some of the colours of tea I have dated.

I hold in my memory certain cups over the years as little vignettes. I could paint them. The high-poured waterfall of mint in Morocco, just as it hits the coloured glass set upon a silver tray. Steam rising from a chipped red mug set on a wall in Cumbria. A full, stone-cold cup on a certain person's kitchen table.

But the most important tea is constantly regenerating. Because the most important tea, whichever flavour, is the first brew of the day. Aaah, it seems to say. Aaah, you repeat. The day has stretched its arms.

POLLING DAY

It cannot be said that voting is a small thing. Democracy is one of the most important things in life, up there with love and art and watching beautiful sunsets. However, there are also the minutiae of the voting process – and that is a true pleasure. The little polling card slipped through the letterbox (even though you don't actually need it). The fact that the polling stations I have been assigned throughout my voting life have been primary schools. The short five-minute walk back into childhood, but with the responsibilities of adulthood. The tiny chairs and tables. The phonebox-sized voting booths. The teensy pencils. The small talk all day in the office, revolving around the question: 'Have you voted yet?'

There is always a weird frisson of excitement on election day – a wholesome sense of doing one's duty. I experience this even when I know the outcome is likely to go against me. It's a strange sort of thing: everyone keeping a secret, together. A conspiracy, but out in the open. Though these days people tend not to keep their votes private or, more often, their politics are obvious. Sometimes I long for a commemorative sticker, I VOTED, like when I got my Covid vaccination.

Some colour code their outfit to the party they are voting for. Obviously, there are the politicians themselves in team-colour ties, but I am thinking more of nineteen-year-olds with red roses painted on their nails. There is the soul-boosting social media trend in recent years of #DogsAt-PollingStations. Grinning dogs with blue or red or yellow rosettes. (What do dog breeds say about a person's politics? I am convinced: something.)

There are the small acts of (slightly self-interested) kindness: people offering lifts to the elderly or those in rural areas. The texts friends send at 9.30 p.m.: 'It's not too late!' The volunteers, far better citizens than me, who give up their time to work the phones and the tellers who conduct informal exit polls.

Then: the nerdiest house parties in existence. The all-nighters pulled, not in cool warehouses with exposed piping and drugs you don't even know the names of, but sat in someone's living room with crisps in bowls and wine in cups watching the swingometer. The flagging at 2 a.m. The second wind at 2.30 a.m. The ironic cheers that go up for the novelty candidates, dressed in costume, who win 233 votes. The three-minute interviews with newly elected MPs, trying to look statesmanlike, in front of gym basketball hoops.

I love every single thing about polling day, even amidst the potential of crushing disappointment. And if the result is the one I long for? Well, that is no small joy. That is a thing of enormous satisfaction indeed.

ANTIQUE
SHOPPING

On the one hand, I am the world's least organised person. On the other, I was buying furniture for my future first home aged thirteen. I am not sure where my love of design and homeware originated. All I know is that while pals were reading *Sugar* and watching *EastEnders*, I was purchasing *Yellow Pages*-sized interiors quarterlies and refusing to miss an episode of *Grand Designs*.

Mostly, this obsession took (and takes) the form of shopping for secondhand, vintage and antique pieces. My earliest 'get' was a huge Guinness pub mirror – somewhat sought after nowadays – that I picked up for £7 in the local charity shop. I bought my first record player at fifteen, a restored number. In beautiful synchronicity, it was a 1960s Fidelity targeted at the teen market.

True contentment is browsing antique shops, flea markets, car boot sales and charity shops. All the better when I stumble across a place I never knew existed in an incongruous location. I used to live in an area mostly populated by chicken shops, old-style internet cafes and drug dealers. But, randomly, in the middle of all this was a wonderful antiques place. Velvet cocktail chairs; opaque-use kitchen appliances; Parker Knoll two-seaters. Tucked-away places and those outside big cities are less expensive and have far more curios. Some sellers scout the same pieces and objects over and over again, which is no fun.

My treasure hunting doesn't merely encompass furniture. I will also excitedly pick up first editions of books; obscure records by artists I have never heard of; things I don't even understand the point of, but that steal my heart.

The internet has changed this habit. One can now browse online marketplaces and end up in a 5 a.m. bidding war for a lightly scratched G-Plan bureau. I'd say the dedicated investigative work that takes place online to seek out something long desired equals that of happening across a wonder in real life.

As we know, however, there is rarely pleasure without pain. As someone who does not drive, I find myself straining muscles I didn't know I had heaving footstools home. Or undermining a bargain by paying through the nose for delivery. But that I can take a stroll and pick up five old Penguin paperbacks for a quid each? Or step out of a shop, door chiming sweetly as I leave, in a long-neglected, ridiculously patterned knitted jumper? That's a vintage pleasure.

SCRATCHING
AN ITCH

First of all, let's get this straight: the itch is the thing you scratch. Itch, to me, is not the verb. Some people think itch is the verb, and I find this almost as uncomfortable as an itch itself. An itch, as we know, is very distressing. But there is nothing more rewarding than a problem solved, and it is my deeply felt belief that one of the finest examples of this is a satisfactorily scratched itch.

I don't mean more pervasive itching: nobody lusts after scabies, painful psoriasis or the kind of eczema that makes life as unbearable as tinnitus; but hitting the spot of that niggling sensation is a moment of pure bliss. Scrabbling up and down the stubbly regrowth of shins; the momentary relief from scalping the heads of holiday midge bites; pressuring your partner into giving you a back rub and making them work a very specific spot between the shoulder blades (left a bit, right a bit), for way longer than they are happy with, resulting in shudders of delight.

Itching is a little like yawning and sneezing, in that it is tied up in the mirror neurone effect. You may even have had a little scratch while reading this article. One study found that people listening to a lecture on itching began to scratch themselves. Everyone appreciates this orgasm of the epidermis (so sorry). If you want to show off, by the way, you can call an itch by its medical name: pruritus.

It isn't just humans who are affected by the urge to scratch, and thank god, because then we would be denied the pleasure of watching pets, fresh from the vet's, walk into walls wearing anti-scratch cones. Then reversing and trying again.

Some enjoy the sensation of scratching not related to the body. But (appropriately named) scratchcards have the opposite effect for me. The sensation of scraping off that silver residue goes through me like nails on a chalkboard. It's dry, rough – and it will only end in disappointment.

The scientific reason why scratching our itches feels so good is because it releases serotonin, the neurotransmitter involved in mood-boosting. It foxes the brain by replacing the itch signals with pain signals (that kind of pleasure-pain). It is pure distraction. And my god, with the world today, don't we need that right now.

TIPSINESS

'Too much of a good thing' is a proverb that I generally disagree with. Alcohol is an exception – for many people and for different reasons, any alcohol is too much. When I went without it for a year, the most radical change was having much more time. The days expanded. Why? Because I was no longer spending half my weekends in bed wishing for a quick death. There are headaches, and then there are hangovers.

I will level with you: 'drinking in moderation' sounds incredibly dull; or strained, when said in the voiceover of booze adverts. You can almost envisage the gun to the head. Not that I am saying there isn't a time and a place for getting wasted. (I do not know the etymology of the British term 'rat-arsed', but I am fond of it – despite the fact that rats are not known to be drunks, and I do not understand what their bottoms would have to do with it if they were.)

The sweet spot is that wonderful word: tipsy. Tipsy captures the brightening of spirits and loosening of the tongue. The easy laughs, the growth in tactility. The bonhomie of good company lubricated by favourite beverages. The backslaps at the bar, or the gathering orders for rounds. Good wine being poured across a dining table. Easily-struck-up rapport with strangers or mutual friends. Pints of beer being cheers'd, or cocktail glasses clinking. Shots as a team sport.

Tipsy is the golden hour. What lies ahead, sometimes, is the danger zone of unwise decision-making; the losing of personal effects; the blurring of eyesight; and, oh god, the potential lurching of the gut and vomiting into a loo bowl. Once we're at that point, the sun has truly set. Dignity is nowhere to be found.

There are times when these unfortunate consequences are worth it for the bacchanalia preceding (my birthday springs to mind), but more often – and especially as one grows older – the true joy is cashing in on the evening at just the right time. This is a difficult skill to acquire because, as with all gambling, the lure of just one more is a strong one.

It is almost never just one more, and ending the night in disarray can bin the recollection of that wonderful warm feeling, two drinks in. Tipsy is what to aim for. Tipsy is the convivial character of an evening perfectly played. Tipsy is your friend. I will drink to Tipsy.

BEING INSIDE WHEN
IT'S RAINING

It's a memory from many of our childhoods: tucked up cosily in sleeping bags, safely inside tents, the patter of rain against canvas overhead. I think it remains one of my favourite sounds. That, along with trees rustling in the wind; the thwacks and clinks and clonks of sports; a wide, flat brush making its way crisply through freshly washed hair; the crackle of flames.

But one doesn't have to be in a tent to appreciate the sound of rain (or under a gazebo; or, as I seem to remember vividly when a toddler, under a plastic pram cover). Or even under an umbrella. The sound of rain pelting a car window, along with the squeak of the windscreen wipers, will do it for me. The bouncing of hailstones off sitting-room windowpanes, muffled slightly by curtains drawn against the winter dark. I especially love the sound of hail pinging off the inside of a chimney chute and hitting the hearth.

Our senses crave juxtaposition. That's why sitting in a sauna and then rolling around in snow is so popular in Russia and elsewhere. It's why a howl of laughter can slip into a sombre reflection before our eyes have fully uncreased. It's why sweet-and-sour chicken exists. And it is why there is nothing better than being ensconced in the warm, comfortable environs of one's home, when outside the roads are wet and the gutters streaming. Who doesn't love turning up the television volume over the rumblings of thunder?

Shaking the water from a brolly and leaving it in the hallway propped up like a satellite dish, jammed in between radiator and skirting board; kicking off boots to slide into slippers – it's all part of the evening nesting routine. Sure, it's still nice to be at home when the weather outside is fine, but the snugness is that little bit extra when it is tipping it down.

You'd be surprised how much great writing about rain there is (a deluge, you might say) but my favourite line is this stunningly sardonic number by Mark Twain: 'The rain is famous for falling on the just and unjust alike, but if I had the management of such affairs I would rain softly and sweetly on the just, but if I caught a sample of the unjust out doors I would drown him.' Either way, my ears are pricked.

MEMES

Social media has a bad reputation, and for good reason: white supremacy left unchecked; revenge porn; livestreaming of mass murder; the spread of fake news, possibly undermining world democracy. It isn't the greatest list.

I quit Facebook long ago. Well, in 2013, which in the internet age counts as long ago. Most social media I keep up with solely for work. But there are times when, for me, despite all its true horror, social media – and memes in particular – induce tears of laughter. What has made me laugh the hardest over the past few years have not been the sold-out Edinburgh fringe shows or the Bafta-winning television comedies, but strangers on the internet.

In the greatest of ironies, it is the mostly unhumorous Richard Dawkins who gave us the word 'meme', which he coined in his 1976 work *The Selfish Gene*. He defined a meme as: 'a unit of cultural transmission', encompassing ideas, symbols and practices. The derivation is the ancient Greek word 'mimeme': imitated thing. It's probable that neither the Greeks nor Richard Dawkins foresaw the internet's Distracted Boyfriend, in which a stock photograph of a man walking hand-in-hand with his partner while checking out another woman – much to his girlfriend's annoyance – has been used as an analogy for everything, from eyeing up new titles in a bookshop while unread ones are neglected at home, to millennials turning their backs on capitalism for socialism.

For a meme to really take off, it has to be relatable; it has to contain a truth universally acknowledged, as Jane Austen would put it. That is basically how all jokes work. What I love about memes is the way they bring out the best in people: their wit, their absurdist thinking, their quick turns of phrase. I love that a seventeen-year-old girl in a Minnesota bedroom can reduce me to belly laughs as much as a father in Norwich or Jakarta. I adore the twists and turns of a meme's journey. It doesn't matter what form they take: TikTok; video clips; Vines (RIP); Snapchat stories; Twitter threads; old-school image macros.

The greatest ones often have a central juxtaposition or an imaginative leap. An old favourite is Unhelpful Teacher, a stock image of a woman in front of a blackboard whose jaunty expression is entirely unrelated to the quotes people make up for her: 'Oh, you don't understand? Let me explain it again in the exact same way.'

Yes, the internet is in many ways driving us apart. But memes are bringing us together.

FREE UPGRADES

They say fortune favours the brave. But what if it favours those who are nice to check-in staff, happen to encounter a hospitality worker in a good mood or are canny enough to hit a market just before it closes?

Sometimes good things do, in fact, come for free. And if there is one thing better than a treat, it is an unexpected one. Finding a fiver in an old jacket pocket feels like winning the lottery. Being the recipient of random human kindness somehow makes one feel shiny, special. Now, I don't wish to sully the wholesome tone by bringing commerce into this, but . . . isn't it the best to get a free upgrade, discount or no-strings-attached offer?

These things can happen purely out of luck. An algorithm plucks you from an electronic list of subscribers to get a year's worth of magazines free. Other times, our behaviour has a role. Staff at Pret are told to give away a certain number of items to customers every week as part of official policy and I have been the beneficiary on many occasions. Free flat whites, free cookies – once even encouragement to take a cookie I hadn't ordered but must have been looking at longingly. Bananas waved away. An extra croissant popped into the bag.

I would like to think that my sparkly, charming personality has had a hand in this; my engaging repartee. But it may possibly be just to stop me talking and get me out of the shop as quickly as possible.

One of the greatest gifts in life is a sea view. I do not understand, therefore, how hotel receptionists keep their egos in control. I would be drunk with power if I had this ability; to bestow something that undoubtedly makes a holiday circa 37 per cent better than if the room you happened to be lumped with faced the hotel's laundry-room, for instance.

I have never had the holy grail of a flight upgrade. I have, however, often been switched to seats with extra leg room on planes and in posh cinemas. I have a jumper that a vintage clothes stallholder once, with a shrug of the shoulders, gave me for free when I was buying another item. It turned out I liked the freebie better than the purchase.

I don't think it is saving money that makes these freebies so happy-making, but the warm feeling you get knowing that someone cares enough, or is generous enough, to want to make your day a little better. Though, obviously, a 70 per cent discount on a laptop is also not to be sniffed at, I'll tell you that for free.

SILENCE

Not many people have heard of misophonia – which is iron-ic, because it has everything to do with hearing. It describes extreme reactions – in my case, mostly rage, but in the case of others it may be anxiety or disgust – to certain sounds. I don't actually know whether I have misophonia. It seems low on the list of conditions I have to worry about, or potentially worry about, but there is no doubt I get disproportionately irritated by certain sounds, all of them human-made.

The issue is that while some sounds are inconsiderate (leaking music from headphones, for instance, which I think most people can't stand), others are socially acceptable. Kids constantly shrieking are just expressing themselves; some-one can't help it if they need to clear their throat repeatedly. The man nonstop clicking his lighter during a bus ride wasn't harming anyone, but I had to politely and apologetically ask him if he would mind stopping, because otherwise I wasn't sure I would end the journey with my nerves intact. I have a two-stage strategy with continuous whisperers in the cinema: a dagger stare, then going over and asking them to shut up.

It will come as no surprise, then, that I find absolute silence almost a divine state. Lying on my back in a cyan sea, both ears underwater, staring up into a sky uninterrupted by clouds, I feel as though every problem I have could sink into the sand and bury itself. Total silence: the world on mute; the chatter of Twitter buttoned as it leaves opinionated mouths.

I don't hate all noise. I even adore some sounds. I enjoy the clack of a keyboard. But being awake during the night, when sound sometimes stops, as though a needle is lifted from a record player, is stunning.

A physicist will say there is no such thing as absolute silence. The lowest sound level in the natural world is that of particles moving through gas or liquid, known as Brownian motion. But tech companies have tried to top this, creating sound-sealed rooms known as anechoic chambers. Apparently, spending forty-five minutes or so in one will make you go a bit mad – it is that quiet. I would still like to know if there are any in the UK that will let me visit.

OVERHEARING

There's a reason why magazines run 'overheard' columns and you find social media accounts dedicated to the same. That humans are capable of saying things so unexpected, bizarre, idiotic, hilarious or filthy is one of the great, simple joys in life.

Strip such remarks from their context and they can indeed be elevated into art. Or perhaps you know the context, but marvel at the opinion or observation. You might let your nostrils flare in mirth or catch the eye of the speaker to signal agreement. Then there is the jaw-drop of something utterly moronic said behind you on public transport. Messaging it to a pal to share the goods. Barking with laughter when remembering it, months later.

Children are great value when it comes to overheards. The New York toddler who waved to a pigeon and said: 'Bye, street chicken!' Or the mother I heard saying to (presumably) her daughter: 'No, betting isn't a job, darling.'

But there are gems in every category, as a website called BoredPanda attests. Sex exchanges: 'Have you ever been handcuffed?' 'Sexually or by law enforcement?' Witty back-and-forths: 'How drunk were you last night?' 'I bought miniature furniture on eBay.' Snarky ones: 'Doesn't she have a tattoo that says "relevant"?' 'Yeah, but it's fading, so that's fitting.' There-but-for-the-grace-of-god ones: 'I was wearing that new camo jacket and someone thanked me for my service.' The tears-inducing, like a woman asking where to find the frozen vegetables and a cashier replying: 'The freezer.' And the woman responding: 'Thank you.'

A Twitter account popular among journalists is @OHnewsroom, for Overheard in the Newsroom. Things I heard in the *Guardian* newsroom and shared with this account include: a colleague remarking they had spent New Year's Eve at L. Ron Hubbard's house; a mix-up between PJ Harvey and Brian Harvey from East 17; and someone saying: 'Just Google "cat, parasite, depression".' I can only imagine.

Why do I keep a note of them? Because overheards provide wonderful material. I heard a man say to his mate at a bar: 'To some people, it's black and white with Nazi criminals.' That one found its way into the mouth of a short-story character.

The phrase is to keep one's ears to the ground. I recommend keeping one's head up, to catch the end of businessmen's back-and-forth; the denouement of an argument; the riffs of reuniting friends. Nuggets of intrigue, comedy, shock. Please go on: I'm listening.

EMPTY CITIES

There are times of the year – the height of the summer holidays or the period between Christmas Day and New Year's Eve – when city roads become bare and the pavements clear. Queues dwindle. Buses proffer seats. The clicks of heels echo around empty underground stations. Breathing in lifts becomes a thing. Running is to run undisturbed.

Living and working in a city is great, but you can't escape the rat-race clichés: escalators of necks craning over phones and commuters rearranging themselves in a suited Rubik's cube to allow a train door to close; the struggle to find a space in a pub and the very British request to 'perch' at the end of someone else's table.

But when the non-native citizens of cities untether themselves from the flat whites, the desk lunches, the club nights, the traffic jams and the naff ads; when the out-of-office responses go on and suitcases are filled with swimming gear, or presents, and rolled on to platforms and stuffed into the boots of taxis: that is the magic. That is the smoothing out of terrain like a new map, revealing things gone unnoticed.

You remember those amazing shots of an empty Westminster Bridge at the beginning of *28 Days Later*? Andrew Macdonald, the film's producer, explained how they achieved

those scenes: by filming in July at 4 a.m., waiting for the sun to come up, grabbing an hour or so of emptiness before rush hour. Before the fumes, the flapping newspapers and the cacophonous soundtrack of city life: barriers beeping, doors hissing, exhaust fumes sputtering.

I will never forget when I spent an entire journey on public transport by myself. Past 11 p.m. on a bank holiday Monday, I was returning from elsewhere as the rest of the capital moisturised, took out their contact lenses and prepared for the return to work. I, meanwhile, boarded a vacant carriage, then alighted at a station without a single soul in it. A mouse scuttled past, but – did I imagine this? – slower than normal.

There are opposites to all of this, of course: the year-round lido swimmer bombarded by fairweather dippers when temperatures hit 27°C. The galleries suddenly packed out by blockbuster exhibitions. The quiet park hosting a funfair. That is when I look forward to time off during school terms and mid-December breaks.

What I am saying is this: I encourage you to take a holiday, but my motives are not entirely altruistic.

STAYING OVER

I can't remember how much I enjoyed – or didn't like – sleep-overs as a child. I suppose it depended on the other guests. They are not something I recall having a strong opinion on. Yet I find staying at friends' houses as an adult immensely pleasurable. In truth, I find staying anywhere rather exciting, and hospitality in general a lovely thing. I occasionally stay in fancy hotels in the city where I live, just for a night, to break up the monotony (and for the rooftop pools).

On trips abroad, I enjoy staying with locals. But there is something specifically satisfying and, more than that, comforting about staying with pals. I'm sure a large part of this is that I somehow have friends with fancy houses in beautiful locations. I have friends with a stunning house in Oxford, mates with quaint cottages by the seaside.

A second factor is that my friends, in general, have their shit together more than I do: a domestic goddess I am not (despite my love of homeware and design). The feeling of being invited into someone else's nest provides a privileged kind of contentment. Friends are the family we choose.

Late-night chatting by the fire and catching up over shared washing-up. Making time for breakfast with fresh orange juice, when the visit is on a weekend. Or mutually pulling on coats and picking up coffee en route to the train if I have crashed on a weeknight.

What I love best, though, is the juxtaposition between the warm familiarity of a friend you know and love, and the subtle high of a twist on the everyday. A different type of toothpaste (is it nicer than yours – fresher?). A shower that works an alternative way. Kitchen utensils you don't own and can't name. It is like snooping in a National Trust house, but one that is lived in by occupants you care about and who aren't racist.

Perhaps the crux of it is: I feel safe. I feel wanted. If someone is willing to make up the spare bed for you, they must hold you in some regard. If someone pops their head round the door to offer you a cuppa in the morning, they can't secretly despise you, right?

Maybe people who come from picture-perfect homes and archetypal nuclear families don't have this joy. Maybe they are spoiled. But for me, there is a special type of bonding in someone saying, 'Of course there is room at the inn.' Of course, I return the favour – but not before warning you about the radiator that makes a super-weird noise in the night.

MASSAGES

It sounds indulgent, and that's because it is, but I adore a massage. I worry that they have been tainted in popular consciousness by creepy co-workers lurking over interns, or sepia memories of adverts in phone boxes promising 'happy endings', or perhaps villains in films casually issuing directives for genocide while face down wearing a towel.

Really, though, is there anything better than a massage that hits the spot, or multiple spots? That kneads knots and soothes skin, pummels away pressure and works out worries?

One has to learn how to be the subject of a good massage. The most important aspect is matching with a good masseur or masseuse (it is similar to finding a suitable psychotherapist). Do you want a talker and, if not, is this person someone you feel comfortable with in silence? I have a habit of filling silences out of awkwardness, even in situations where it is perfectly acceptable not to speak – and if you are filling a silence out of awkwardness, that is not relaxing.

Also, will your therapist bring up truly out-there alternative medicines that verge on conspiracy theory? Again, not relaxing.

Deciding on the type of massage (Swedish, sports or deep tissue?) and location (home or parlour?) is another consideration. I would never enjoy a massage in my home because I know I'd end up noticing a flaking skirting board or books wearing coats of dust. Plus, a folding table would remind me of an ironing board and that, again, is not relaxing.

I much prefer the trickling water features and being offered tea on arrival, despite the fact that there is never time to drink it; I like statues of Buddha that seem offended at their environs. My massage place is next door to my hairdresser, so I make a double trip (massage first, otherwise the oil greases up my haircut).

The final thing is to become comfortable with one's body. I have learned not to care if I have a blemish where a bra strap has rubbed or my legs aren't shaved, or the underwear I am wearing is practical.

Massage is thousands of years old, and crosses cultures and continents, so there must be something in it. I'm no fan of its grand medicinal claims; but there is also no peer-reviewed paper on why an almond Magnum makes me feel good, and I don't question that it does. After a good massage, the world always seems lighter, as do I.

CHOCOLATE

Some people are allergic to chocolate. It's possible that who-ever came up with the axiom 'to count one's blessings' had just learned of this. Others apparently just don't 'like' choco-late, which, if true (I maintain suspicion), there really ought to be some kind of support group.

I go through phases with chocolate. I always like it, but, similar to whichever spot in the house the cat chooses to sleep in, my preference changes. A classic bar of Cadbury Dairy Milk is a current favourite. Breaking the squares off seems almost a subversion of a bread-related religious act – and especially because I'm not sharing it.

As a kid I loved a Milkybar, though the standard bars are as thin as their foil wrappers. Nowadays, white chocolate makes me feel a little sick, although not so sick that I won't greedily swallow the white star from that ubiquitous Tesco chocolate birthday cake. You know the one. By law, one's age does not change unless the Tesco chocolate birthday cake has been served. There are people walking around, full of their mum's homemade cake or years' worth of Waitrose Victoria Sponge, having no idea why their car insurance is still so high.

Sponge, lemon drizzle and red velvet are all good cakes. But chocolate is the indulgent best. With its thick, rich but familiar icing, chocolate cake is casually deluxe in the manner of a fur coat slung over the back of the sofa.

The truly pompous chocolate is dark. Dark chocolate whispers green leathered roll-top desks. Imported rugs and bathtubs with feet. People claim to dislike it because it's bitter, but the key is homing in on prime percentage. For me, that's 70 per cent cocoa. 70 per cent is good bitter, like the fizzy bite of champagne that sneaks in alongside the sweetness. I have a friend who swears by 90 per cent, which is insane.

Its opposite is 'advent calendar chocolate' as I call it: the cheap and cheerful variant that comes in the form of edible coins and baubles. Or in packets picked up in foreign street markets with knock-off names. This chocolate is a rentable city bike; fun for a stint but not a proper vehicle. The dumb boyfriend of chocolate.

Selection boxes cause much anguish: I want it all but get worried about hurting the feelings of the ones I pick late. (NB. I am not claiming this is normal.) Meanwhile, Terry's Chocolate Orange and After Eight Mints speak to me of Christmas but are at least available all year round, should the fancy take (and here a pointed and disapproving glance at Creme Eggs).

The only chocolate I see no need for is liqueur. These just seem to me the world's smallest and least satisfying shots. Oh, and Aero. Aeros, are, quite literally, a waste of space. Plus, they have the consistency of decades-old mortar. Still, it's chocolate. So I'm not going to say no.

DAY TRIPS

OK, let's get the bad out of the way: the portmanteau 'day-cation', a monstrous offshoot of the almost-equally offensive 'staycation'. Given that I believe day trips are twelve-hour delights, they do not deserve to be labelled in such a painful way.

Wherever one lives, and whatever one feels about that place, there is never a downside to going on a miniature jaunt. It's a means of experiencing the world in bitesize; broadening one's horizons, but not too much. If the trip goes badly, it doesn't matter, because: a) it is short and b) it has the effect of casting a new light on one's regular environment.

One thing wealthy people do not understand about those with lesser financial means (and judge them for) is how they manage to – shock horror – own mobile phones, or laptops, or things that cost a few bob. What they are missing is that people who can't afford never-ending luxuries will focus on treats to make the mundane bearable. Big treats saved up for, perhaps, or indulgences little and often.

Most of us cannot afford always to take five-star holidays to white sands and waters as clear as vodka, but day trips to British pebbles or birch trees or historical cities are in reach.

There are multiple thrills. The planning itself is exciting.

Firing up Google Maps; browsing whatever the place has to offer and drafting an itinerary, bookmarks galore. I want to visit art galleries, swim in the sea, eat Victoria sponge and sip at hand-warming coffee, pose outside National Trust homes as though I live there. I'll admit I've never pulled off being 'good' at museums. I guess I like my history to be under my feet, on location, or on the pages of a book.

Though compiling the list of things to do (TripAdvisor reviews read; Instagram pictures scouted) is part of the fun, even more so is following one's nose once there. Sometimes, a trip will be so successful it might spill overnight. This is even more likely when with close pals, who make the best companions for these explorations. (This level of spontaneity depends on the company. New lover? Tired children?)

Domestic holidays fell out of fashion with the advent of budget flights; especially the trips to seaside towns that Victorians enjoyed so much. But with a crappy economy, our time-poor lifestyles, and flight-shaming in the light of a climate crisis – not to mention A PANDEMIC – I'd argue the great British jaunt is on the rise again. So, see you at a bus station in the hinterland, checking timetables.

GIG ENCORES

They say you should always leave people wanting more. And you should, but not too much more. People need to be sated, which is why phrases such as 'full of joy' exist.

This is especially the case when it comes to live music. If I go to a gig and there is no encore, I will be pissed off. I will give that band a poor review – if not professionally, then in my head. Not much tops the euphoria of an encore at the end of a fantastic gig: the feeling of everyone's needs being met at the same time – sort of like an orgy, but with (possibly) stickier floors; the ripples of anticipation through the crowd; the call from stomping feet, the unanimous cheer. You know it's coming, but we also know that the sun sets every day, and that doesn't make it any the less beautiful.

Conversely, is there a greater disappointment than your favourite song being missed off a setlist and then having it not appear in the encore? There is not.

The best encores happen at those gigs that acts have billed as their last ever. I'm a huge Girls Aloud fan and I went to their last ever gig in my home city of Liverpool. True, Sarah spent most of it looking furious and pulling out her earpiece, but their banging pop catalogue still built to an emotional send-off. When the Maccabees, who provided the soundtrack to one of my formative love affairs, played out of their skins for a permanent goodbye at Alexandra Palace in London, I would defy anyone not to have felt moved by the sight of thousands of people pogoing to a song about a swimming pool (Latchmere, in south London), before gulping down the finale, 'Pelican'.

Festival encores can be even more intense: at 2019's Glastonbury, tens of thousands of people poorly rapping Stormzy lyrics back to him. Then there are the finales you wish you could have been at: Queen's last ever performance with Freddie Mercury at Knebworth in 1986, where they played their encores and then Freddie left the stage, wearing a crown, to the national anthem.

To be sure, gigs can go on too long. But for the most part, I would challenge anyone not to come away from a perfectly executed gig finale, streaming out of the gates and the rabbit warren of venue corridors, with a racing heart and a smile, exhilarated and inspired.

PERFECT PENS

It is one of my greatest concerns that, with the ubiquity of tech, I now have the handwriting ability of Edward Scissorhands. I found myself composing a note to my neighbours recently and it took three attempts to make it legible. I used to carry a Moleskine around with me, as all writers should. Now, I just have my phone. This can be uncomfortable when it looks like I am rudely texting while someone is talking when I am in fact making notes.

As a child, I was such an obnoxious show-off that I recall attempting cursive – joined-up writing – while my classmates were practising print letters. Unfortunately, I made the mistake of joining up not only the letters, but the words too, so an entire four-page story resembled the rolling waves of the sea. The shame is still with me.

Over time, my handwriting changed from a tween style that looked like blown bubble-gum to intensely scribbled, squished missives. My lowercase 't' transformed into a crucifix and my ampersands were a blasé loop. My love of writing was connected with the act of physically marking things. I wrote everywhere: on the backs of fag packets, inside cereal boxes, the margins of newspapers, my skin. The most enjoyable aspect of writing? (Apart from, perhaps, writing something good?) Writing with the perfect pen. I don't mean a £350 Mont Blanc, because if you are writing with a £350 pen I will assume you are a banker and responsible for a lot of what is wrong with the world. I am talking about the mighty uni-ball eye. This is one of the world's most ubiquitous pens, adored for both its cushioned grip and its rollerball that glides across paper.

Many people swear by the perfect fountain pen, and I admit to liking their quill-esque nature, but I was scarred early on by having repeated leaks in school bags. (Also by having to wash my hands to a Lady Macbeth degree after using.)

I'm sure it isn't true that words are better when inked, and whenever I hear of authors insisting on writing manuscripts by hand, I repress an eye-roll. But it's a bit like when I change the typeface on Google Docs: one minute I've written something banal, then suddenly, after switching from Arial to Georgia, I am a genius. I don't miss the wrist ache, but I do miss the scratch and scrape of a loyal friend. My kink is ink.

REGIONAL ACCENTS

I am from Liverpool, so am well versed in regional accents. Mine was never pronounced (so to speak) and, after living abroad, then Oxford and now London, it slip-slides; a baby deer on ice. Often people narrow their eyes at me, trying to work out where I am from. It may be unplaceable but as soon as I go back to Liverpool and spend time around scousers, it tends to pick up again.

This is something called the chameleon effect. We subconsciously mirror people's accents and body language to fit in. It is not copying, but a natural reflection.

A question often asked is how one pronounces neither or neither, either or either. But for most of us it's often . . . either. This is true of many words for me. Down south, the long 'a' rules in bath or laugh or glass. The north has flat, short vowel sounds. I never really know which type of 'a' is going to come out of my mouth.

I like the Liverpudlian accent's melodic cadence, which lends itself to the humour the city is famed for. But I wouldn't say it was my favourite. I feel a solidarity with brummies, because the accent is disparaged as much as the scouse one.

I do like received pronunciation, although apparently it is spoken by only 2 per cent of the population – and 99.9 per cent of BBC presenters. The Queen's speech, I'm so sorry, has come to sound absurd, with a touch of the Bond villain. I wouldn't want the upper classes to dilute their accents, however; I don't think anybody should be coerced in such a way.

I really was not a fan of cockney – but then along came Adele. Glaswegian is great.

But my favourite accent is to be found in Belfast; a Northern Irish accent immediately adds three points to a person's attractiveness. It has the friendliness of scouse but is much softer and more charming.

I used to have an ex-girlfriend who, I'm ashamed to say, I frequently asked to say 'power shower'. She was not, she told me many times, 'a performing monkey'. But whenever she relented, I soaked in that 'power shower' just as I would a deeply pleasurable, relaxing bath. And how, then, did you pronounce that final word?

SETTING THE
OUT-OF-OFFICE

When one thinks of the glorious anticipation of a holiday, packing comes to mind. However, being a perennially disorganised person who would probably have made the journey to Mordor with the ring and nothing else – in fact, possibly not even the ring – this is never a key part of the prep for me. I'll make sure I have swimming gear, or thermals; whichever is required. Mostly, I will be faff-free.

There are things that set the vacation pulse racing: letting the passport off its desk-drawer leash, for instance. But there is only one virtual equivalent of kicking off the brogues and slipping on the flip-flops: setting the out-of-office.

There are many different styles of out-of-office (to those in marketing, it is always the OOO). I'm sure there exists a magazine quiz: What Does Your OOO Say About You?

If you are someone with a proper job, your message probably includes contact details of other people to bother in your absence. These people will not be thrilled. Some out-of-offices are very blunt: 'I am away and back on x date. I will be deleting all messages sent in the interim', being a particular favourite I've encountered. Others are circumspect, in the 'I can't get to the phone right now' landline-voicemail vibe of yore. In case someone tried to . . . hot desk? Steal your charger?

My own used to read politely that I was not around and gave the date I'd be back looking at emails. But . . .people still email. People will never not email. Just checking in again!!! Just circling back!!!

Now, my out-of-office is simply: me <------ distance------> the office. My auto-reply might as well be a photograph of me in a hammock. Which is actually quite a good idea.

It is entering those dates, that sliver of calendar year, that marks the true coming of the holiday spirit. Bury the inbox in the sands of the Sahara. Drown it in Lake Garda. Chuck it off the Cornish coast. Nobody can 'reach out' now. You are safe.

GOOD COFFEE

Reading an Anna Wintour interview, I am afraid I was disappointed by a certain reveal (and I use the word 'reveal' loosely, as I was widely mocked by friends who said this was a well-known fact): Wintour drinks Starbucks coffee. Anna Wintour, the world's chicest. Drinks Starbucks. Not the worst ever coffee, but a close second, behind Costa (it should be criminalised). In the same interview, Wintour talked about playing tennis with her good friend Roger Federer. Starbucks. You can see the discrepancy here.

Anyway, those friends responded with 'duh' and an eye-roll when I mentioned this. Had I never seen *The Devil Wears Prada*? Or *The September Issue*? I've seen both, but maybe I blocked the Starbucks cups from my mind.

I, too, used to drink copious amounts of Starbucks, but that was when I drank lattes, or, as my friend calls them, 'giant cups of milk'. I am now a flat-white girl and take my coffee more seriously.

The problem with good coffee is that once it grasps the taste buds with the vigour of a newborn grasping a lock of hair, it is difficult to go back to any old sludge. I have managed to cut my intake down to two a day: I carry them around in a luminous reusable cup and sup at my anti-fatigue elixir once in the morning and again after lunch. Of course, I know that giving up caffeine is supposed to make one more energised – but it's no longer just about the hit.

If I am not working in the office, I go to one of my favourite cafés and drink a (Fairtrade) Colombian blend, and revel in the fact I am consuming something that, while bringing me much pleasure, is not as bad for me as so many other things I might be ingesting.

Don't get me wrong: I am not so obsessed that I have spent a lot of money I cannot afford on a home espresso machine. But I am at the stage where, if I don't think the coffee will be up to scratch, I order tea. I have grown out of bad coffee. It doesn't have to be from a fancy place; there is a kiosk close to my nearest station that sells great coffee. An Italian man owns it, naturally. (PS: Try ordering a 'latte' in Italy, where it just means 'milk'.) I am not sure it is true that brewing coffee before showing a potential buyer around your home increases the likelihood of a purchase, as is claimed, but reader: I can 100 per cent believe it.

NIGHT BUSES

I apologise for introducing the doom of depression into meditations on the joys of small things, but it was in the middle of a quagmire of ennui, nocturnal sleeping patterns and the cold winds of increasing isolation – familiar to many who experience mental health problems – that this particular delight was discovered. It's a slim one, but critical. A delight that, when I am most well, I do not experience. It is riding buses at night.

Night buses are synonymous with drunken, rowdy revellers; takeaway food in polystyrene containers; the stink of skunk; amusing group banter overheard. But night buses midweek, when the sky is the colour of plums and the only other road users are maintenance workers – those night buses are a different prospect altogether.

When I am deeply depressed, I sleep a lot. The opposite of the usual. I can sleep for twenty hours a day when at my most despairing. I'll wake up at midnight or so, when all over the country novels are slipping from the grasp of married couples propped up by pillows, glasses are removed, bedside lights snapped off. I wake up hungry and alone and pathetic.

In London, in the heart of Soho, there is a café that's open twenty-four hours a day. I pull on jeans and a jumper, close my flat door behind me – a slow, quiet click. Catching the bus at circa 2 a.m., you can almost hear the wheels turn on the road. The driver will nod and perhaps wonder at your story. Mostly, the buses are empty. Many times, an entire journey has, start to finish, accommodated me as the only passenger. Occasionally, on the back seat, the hidden homeless sleep, or medics alight, bleary-eyed.

I head, always, to the front seats. Either I read (I read the entirety of Sally Rooney's *Conversations with Friends* on the 24 bus) or, more often, track the deserted streets while listening to music. Bowie; Cat Power; James Blake; Johnny Cash. Wondering what it would be like to shoot a man in Reno just to watch him die. Thinking about the turns that life takes. Turning the corner at the hospital where you yourself almost died, but didn't; appreciating the buildings that have survived all that technology has thrown at them. The bus waits at red lights for ghosts.

I have done some of my best thinking on night buses. The feeling of going from A to B, of having some kind of destination, when all else has ground to a halt. At the café, the waiters greet me warmly, as a regular who has the cover story that she works nights, but who is almost certainly lying. I eat pancakes in a moat of syrup and sip at tea. I chat to them when I haven't seen friends in weeks. And afterwards, the drivers of the night buses see I get back home safe.

MINT

Mint is the most versatile thing in the world. You might say, 'But what about a little black dress, which can go with anything?', or you might suggest footballers who can play in multiple positions, sometimes all at once. No, sorry: it's definitely, without a shadow of a doubt, mint.

I am not alone in this opinion. The journalist Eleanor Margolis recently said something similar on Twitter, and 250,000 people hit the like button. That's a lot of mint fans. 250,000 is almost as many as there are uses for mint.

'Refreshing' is the word most associated with this masterful herb, as it is truly a life force. Use a mint shower gel and you feel reborn, ready to take on anything. Have it in a mojito, nestled next to crushed ice, and it's a perfect pick-me-up. Have it in a hot cup of water for a soothing tea. I don't understand how something that can make you feel fully ready for the coming day, burstingly alive, can also prepare you for sleep; but that is the magic of mint.

You can have it with eggs. You can clean your teeth with it. You can make a sauce that sings on roast potatoes. You can rub it on your chest to help you breathe easier, or chew it to make your breath better. It's delicious in chocolate. Delicious in ice-cream. Some even like it in cigarettes (absolutely not, but each to their own).

In certain parts of the UK, 'that's mint' means something is good. In Poland, 'to feel mint' can mean to be in love. Which makes sense, given the quasi-high both induce. I feel fresher and cleaner even writing this.

It tastes like heaven, it smells like heaven, it feels like heaven. Mint is very much heaven. It is notorious for muscling out every other plant in a garden – and I wouldn't have it any other way.

THE FINAL DAB
OF PAINT

If you really want to experience the glory of paint, the thick swell it can cause in the heart, I'd recommend seeing a Frank Auerbach in the flesh. Failing that, acquiring one of his books. I consume art as some sweep the shelves of pharmacies for multivitamins. Throw it down my throat like a shot. While I can appreciate the intricacies of a charcoal sketch and the calming sensations of a watercolour, it is the slathered fat waves of oil and acrylic that are my drugs of choice.

I doodled constantly as a child and a teenager, almost compulsively. Every breath I took, out popped a ballpoint portrait of a guy with floppy hair, a woman with architectural cheekbones or an imagined plant with invented shapes for leaves. I no longer doodle because my hands have been commandeered by keyboards and trackpads.

But I do paint. That is when my hands remind me of their dexterity. The lure of paint has yet to dry. Time is suspended when smearing canvas. If one is fully focused, one is untouchable and could be living through almost any period of history. The world has evolved so much that this can be said of fewer and fewer activities. John Keats was not bombing couplets into his Notes app before he forgot them.

Reading, strolling, painting, kissing, crying, napping for

entire afternoons: these are all heritage pursuits. What a thrill to know that I have wiped the paint from bristles with turps in the same manner, or almost, as Vermeer or Van Gogh. Suffered the same multicoloured nail beds for days. Thrown a cloth down in despair. Accidentally wiped navy blue across my forehead. Mixed a colour to match my mood. Nailed a shadow or an earlobe on the fifth attempt.

But the greatest joy of painting is the finish, similar to a marathon or that other popular climax. Transitioning from achieving to achievement. Standing back and thinking: The End. And being content. A dollop of equanimity; a stroke of satisfaction. The tap of wood on wood as the paintbrush returns to the easel. In the beautiful French film *Portrait of a Lady on Fire*, Héloïse asks of her painter lover, 'When do we know it's finished?'

'At one point,' Marianne replies, 'we stop.' It's in the instinctive knowing when to stop that gratification lies.

A SUNDAY ROAST

I once had a friend – and I use the past tense conspicuously – who, when I suggested a walk and a pub Sunday roast, told me she didn't like Sunday roasts. *Did not like Sunday roasts.* I don't know the specific medical terminology for this pathology, but I hope she is getting the help she needs. I imagine so, because the waiting list must be very short.

I'm never happier than when diving into a moat of gravy. If it were possible, I would shrink myself and jump merrily into the middle of a giant, squishy Yorkshire pudding, like a kid on a bouncy castle.

Originally the roast was an after-church meal (hence the Sunday). I think often about how frustrating it is that such a a delight is limited to just one day of the week, and where this ranks on the world scale of injustice (high).

Brits are such big fans of the roast that, in one survey about what we are most proud of, the roast came in at No. 16. Yorkshire puds alone came in at No. 9. To put this into context, that's ahead of Stonehenge, the Royal family and Shakespeare.

As a vegetarian, I am sometimes accused of not taking full advantage of all the roast has to offer, whether that's beef, lamb, pork, chicken, turkey or other meats. But this ignores the fact that the increasing quality of available nut roasts and butternut squash wellingtons tempts even carnivores. It is not uncommon for me to find, these days, that the veggie roasts have run out. (I am sure you can imagine my reaction.) There are also cookbooks and columns full of home options: Nigella's roast stuffed pumpkin or Nigel Slater's parsnip loaf.

Of course, as with the best meals, the joy of a Sunday roast isn't merely about what is on one's plate. It is the act of gathering, and the company one shares. Whether it is a friend hosting and pulling a disparate collection of chairs together to accommodate pals around a too-small table, or meeting up one-on-one with an old mate one hasn't seen for ages, tucking into potatoes and life events. For me, the best roasts are enjoyed after an appetite has been built up on a muddy stroll. The afternoon is spent reading at home, top trouser button undone. Utterly sated.

Or perhaps not quite sated, given how handy the surplus can be to fold into bubble and squeak, or sandwiches. Truly, the gift that keeps on giving. And a deserving matter of national pride.

FIXING THINGS

Mending is back in fashion. As more of us wake up to the 1.2 billion tonnes of carbon produced by the global fashion industry annually, the impact of our wardrobes on the environment is getting harder to ignore. Harder than hiding, on the back hangers, that ugly but expensive top you wore a single time.

I messed about during home economics and textiles lessons at school. I messed about in most lessons, in fairness, but particularly when it came to learning to use a sewing machine. Put one in front of me and it might as well be the Enigma machine.

Now, sewing and knitting are increasingly common pursuits. I am in awe of friends who conjure The Vampire's Wife-style dresses from their own fingers, and patch up hole-ridden sweaters, eschewing new purchases; swapping patterns online and carrying needles around in their bags like paperbacks.

I remain awful at all the above, yet have come to truly appreciate the satisfaction in making and mending. Especially: fixing. I have always loved solving problems. When I moved into my flat, I refused to be beaten by a narrow doorframe when it came to a Chesterfield sofa. A trial-and-error process of angles followed. For hours. This perseverance extends to fixing things.

My solutions aren't exactly kosher, but I don't care a jot, as long as they have the desired effect. Sorting a loose connection in a remote by shoving the foil from a chewing-gum wrapper in there; good as new. Noticing that two loose floorboards in my kitchen are cold on the feet, and stuffing newspaper in the gaps. Similarly, folded napkins under a wobbly restaurant table.

This isn't fixing things in the traditional way, i.e., properly. I'm not saying that taping an extension cord to the back of a desk is the stuff of restoration experts putting together smashed Ming dynasty vases, but I'll still stand back, hands on hips and admire my work, smacking palms together after a job well done. Actually, not well done. But done.

People more skilled than I am (read: almost everyone) will no doubt take gratification from repairing punctured tyres or reupholstering a chair, saving it from the indignity of the skip. All I know is, I am a champ when it comes to my innovative ways of repairing. In my head, I build cities from ruins and there is a vast relish in that.

LOCAL GRAFFITI

There is the kind of graffiti or street art that breaks out and goes on to bigger and better things. The Banksy works that are removed from their place of birth and sold for hundreds of thousands, for instance, or the murals on the West Bank wall.

What I'm infatuated with is the more discreet, local graffiti; spontaneous doodles found in unexpected places. The messages that can make visits to the loo a reading experience almost as pleasurable as sitting in a library scouring quirky book annotations: a scrawled observation that the design of a coat hook resembles a drunk octopus; the hidden confession of unrequited love; the country's legislature taken to task via marker pen.

Even better are the dialogues. I have seen, on more than one occasion, questions posed about relationships that have been answered in separate handwriting: 'Dump him!', 'Girl, you deserve better'. I love inspiring quotes, too – the sort that if posted to Instagram might cause me to eye-roll, but somehow, etched against the grain of a stall, speak to me.

On one summer day, the temperature hitting 29°C, I saw a sign that had been changed from: 'This road will be closed for temporary roadworks' to 'for a temporary beach'. The idea made me smile. A road round the corner had been pedestrianised a couple of years back, while a bridge was being repaired, and it had naturally morphed from a rat-run into a space for neighbourly parties and kids' play. The metal street sign peeling off a wall daubed with 'fix me' also has a community spirit.

I enjoy spotting recurring graffiti. Far and wide across London, the words 'Nat has herpes' are scribbled on various surfaces, from bus stops to subways. Nobody knows who Nat is, or whether she really does suffer from such a malady. It's been mooted that one person could not have been responsible for all instances and that it has become a copycat situation. The phrase never has the tinge of a sexist slur, rather the air of a friend taking the piss. Now it has been elevated to part of the urban fabric.

The corporate-commissioned graffiti represents the worst of street art. But the witticisms, heartfelt sentences and subversive acts from fellow humans are a boon. My favourite from the past week? The person who had added in the female actors' names on a film poster, when only the men in the image had billing. Thank you.

BINGEING ON
BOXSETS

A hallmark of living in times of rapid technological advance-
ment is the fast obsolescence of formats. VHS and cassettes
lasted, at least to my memory, for aeons. But not that long
after the iPod's mass-market introduction of the click wheel
– which seemed almost as momentous as the invention of the
actual wheel – did that click come to be seen as clunky. The
MiniDisc arrived on the scene and then left as quickly as a
swimmer overestimating the temperature of a pool.

Physical boxsets, which jostled in my bedroom with shelf
space for similar-sized Russian tomes, have long since been
resigned to bins in charity shops. For a while, I was signed up
to a DVD-rental delivery service – which is also how Netflix
began.

Though they've moved into original programming, the
widespread appeal of Netflix, Amazon, Disney+ (and iPlayer,
All4 et al) remains their vast back catalogues of content. It is
ridiculously easy to re-watch old favourites or dig into cultural blind spots. Then there are all the shows now releasing
entire seasons in one fell swoop; the streaming binge-watch
is the natural evolution to the boxset. It's how I watched *I
May Destroy You; It's A Sin; Normal People* and more.

There is something all-consuming about binge-watching

television – and I mean that in a positive way. When you spend time consistently with characters and setting, the viewing experience is different than when it is staggered. Just as if you saw one friend more often than another you would consider them closer; characters who you are spending significant amounts of time with became a stronger presence in one's life. The universe of that show becomes a second world lived in and not a place occasionally visited. It's the definition of escapism. Television watched all in one go is more akin to the reading experience.

How a show is consumed alters the viewing experience, too. Recently I binge-watched *A Teacher*, its one short season consisting of ten 30-minute episodes, and the intensity of rapid-fire watching suited it. I'm not sure weekly instalments, complete with cliff-hangers, would have worked so well – or even that I would have stuck with it.

Just as the final ever episode of *Schitt's Creek* aired and was lauded, I watched all six seasons of it back to back. *Schitt's Creek* is the perfect example of a show with warm characters and a setting which is easy for the viewer to become heavily invested in; and spending as much time as I did in that world means I totally understand why it has become so adored, and when I finished the finale it felt like a friend moving away.

Even so, I know that all I need to do is open my laptop and find another show – whatever genre – to indulge in, and I'll once again be transported elsewhere . . .

THE SOUNDS OF
SPORTS

Nothing pleases me more than the sounds of sports. I'd narrow it down to a specific one – a specific noise, or a specific sport – but all bring me equal amounts of contentment. Skateboarding is essentially a piece of music to me. There's the clink of the metal of the trucks against the metal lip of a half-pipe; the scrape of the underside of the deck sliding down a handrail; the hollow-sounding roll of plastic wheels against tarmac; the thud of a trick landing. As a teenager, I used to play Tony Hawk's *Pro Skater 2* on the original PlayStation, and I would toggle the soundtrack off, just so I could listen to these in-game sounds. Don't get me wrong, though – I cannot skateboard. But that doesn't matter.

The squeak of a trainer on a gym floor, which I know others can't bear, will take me straight back to school netball: the satisfying swish of the net as a shot pays off. And is there anything as beautiful to the ear as the thwack of a tennis ball, or the crack of a cricket bat? A shuttlecock whipping through the air? The scuttle of boot studs on changing-room floors? The heavy clonk of two snooker balls colliding? There is not. I could watch Olympic skating for ages, not for the shapes, but for the growling carving of the ice.

I am not sure why I find these sounds so delightful, but

it might have something to do with autonomous sensory meridian response (ASMR), the phenomenon that results in 'low-grade euphoria' – or, as I put it, less dramatically, 'a nice tingly feeling' – from various visual or auditory stimuli. I respond to many sounds in this way: hair being cut; fountain pen on paper; the tapping of a keyboard. Sometimes I try to soothe myself to sleep by watching YouTube videos of these things. That sounds weird, but I promise, these videos have millions of views and not all of them are me. There's been research and everything.

But the sounds of sports are special in that they can be as invigorating as they are relaxing. Rattle the crossbar with a volley and pounce on the rebound. Catch the ball on the edge of the racket and listen to the plasticky backhand-save match point. Grab the baseball with a leather mitt – booph! – to win the game.

The only sounds of sports I don't love are those made by people. The parents on the sidelines, red-faced, screaming, 'Man on!' to their twelve-year-old daughters. The awkward arguments with umpires at Wimbledon, every curse audible amid the polite silence of the crowd. The chants on the terraces – you know the ones. All I want is the roulette sounds of the golf ball rolling around the bottom of the hole.

PHARMACISTS

I'm sure a visit to a pharmacy is not a key event for most people. A repeat prescription. Or your hay fever is playing up. Maybe you long for the discounted perfume of pop singers, or three scrunchies in a bargain bin. The kid will eat only the squishy vitamins.

But I love pharmacies. I have never in my entire life met a pharmacist I did not like. Is it in their blood? Is being an exceptional person part of the training? I do not know what I would have done, or would do, without them.

I go to pharmacies a lot because I take a lot of medication. I should rattle when I walk. I know intimately the sizes and shapes of generics (Route 66 sign; hexagon; nuclear bomb) and the melodic ring of the door as I enter the church of indigestion pills, eczema creams and hair dye.

I have written before about the joy of being a regular, and my local pharmacists are the apex. A slice of cake in a café is lovely, but it doesn't silence the noises in my head; or calm the inflammation in my gut; or provide relief from staring at walls at 4 a.m., willing myself to sleep. I even have a yearly NHS subscription card – fancy.

My pharmacists know me. I joke with them. (A particularly well-packed parcel of pills: 'Can you do my Christmas wrapping?') They accept without annoyance my keen curiosity on price gouging and patents. ('Could you just check on the system? I'm intrigued.')

I'm a little bit more with it now, but a previous pharmacist knew that I would always arrive to pick up new medication on the day I had run out. Often, there would not be enough tablets left to fill the prescription, so he would advance an emergency few. He would sigh amiably and potter off into the back.

The compassion on display is a marvel. I imagine that every single public-facing job comes with days of snappiness or tedium, and yet I do not see it in this group of people, who run their fingers down shelves as though in a library searching for a specific book.

I envy the people of Wales and Scotland for their prescription-charge freedom; but the NHS offers great value. Private prescriptions are charged at about a tenner or more (my pharmacist: 'Posh now, are we?' when I handed over a private script). Please join me in raising a luminous pink glass of Pepto-Bismol to the friendliest, most helpful drug dealers you will meet.

THE MOMENT
AFTER WAKING

Each morning upon waking, before I open my eyes, I like to pretend the passing cars are waves. They come in steady rushes on the road below my window, evenly spaced by the speed bumps. If I listen with the correct balance of imagination and concentration, I am on a beach somewhere far, far from home.

People talk of that brief, disorienting flicker that can occur when waking: where am I? A sort of GPS failure in the liminal space between the unconscious and conscious states. I love this moment. It means I could be anywhere and anyone. I am Louis' queen waking in a king-sized Versailles bed. I am swinging into life from a hammock beneath absurd azure skies. I am stirring from a nap after winning multiple prizes, which is a tiring affair.

Quite aside from the opportunity this moment affords for fantasy – before the day's unread banalities come crashing into the brain's inbox – it has other benefits. If, despite not being five, you are still prone to nightmares, as I am, then waking will offer respite; escape from whatever monster sought your head between its jaws, or the crosshairs of a gun that was aimed at you. If the dream was pleasant, the sudden tip back into reality is bittersweet. But it's nice to languidly stretch one's body while analysing the imaginary excursion and dwell on what might have been. You can't truly appreciate the dream while in the dream; it's the seconds after it that count for most.

Of course, for chronic insomniacs, waking up is always going to be a little like dropping a pound coin down a drain. Nothing to be celebrated. So it is true that often my first thought upon waking is to go back to sleep. And if that is possible, there is joy in that, too.

There is a different, and unfortunately all too rare, bliss in waking up to the realisation that one has had a perfect, dreamless sleep: deep, sound and lengthy. A sleep like this and I'd win the Tour de France on a tricycle.

As it goes, I won't know what it's like to win the Tour, even on a regular bike. Except if I were to dream about it: in that moment of waking, when I'll be able to feel the metal's imprint on my skin; the taste of sweat on my upper lip. Those moments as sleep dissipates, and either the life of the dream is tangible, or time seems shaken out, taut and new.

MASTERING A
NEW SKILL

It is 5 a.m. and the roads are silent; the air sharp and steady from the overnight respite. No fumes and clashing horns and rumbling of lorries; no exhaust-pipe mushroom clouds in miniature. At 5 a.m., everything is still, and I am alone. These are the only reasons I am out at this hour.

You see, along with everyone else, I decided to get a bike during lockdown. I was far too late to take full advantage of the vacant streets, hence my workaround solution.

After fighting a number of people to the death and passing a ritualistic initiation ceremony that involved fingerless gloves but about which I am not allowed to say more, I arrived at Halfords to pick up a Zelos, which I figured was good, because zelos means zeal. (There is a model called Vengeance in the same range, which I did not trust myself with.) I knew nothing else because I have not ridden a bike in almost a decade.

'Starting is the hardest part' is an acknowledged truism, and everyone recognises the glory of a silverware triumph. What people rarely mention is the sheer satisfaction of nailing the bit after the starting. Mastering the basics.

This is a quantum leap: a sudden, tiny jump that has drastic effects. It's the feeling of suddenly getting a particular

technique or movement or step and wondering how we ever found it impossible.

For me, this gained foothold is a greater pleasure than big achievements in areas I am already good in. Footholds is an apt term, because realising I should be letting my legs do the majority of the work in bouldering was a breakthrough. Conversely, after watching YouTube swimming videos on how to improve my tragic front crawl, I learned that the legs, basically, do very little. I can easily remember myself as a frustrated schoolgirl, transformed by grasping theories set out by long-ago dead men via the conduit of a Year 6 teacher. (I imagine the teachers share that buzz.)

So, I am up at 5 a.m. to practise the different gear systems on a road bike and to conquer . . . staying on it. I am not entirely alone. There is a fox, whom I have named Dave. Dave sits and watches as I go up and down a particular street before I get nervous that my clunking chain will wake its inhabitants and move to another. Nobody but Dave is there to see me signal into nonexistent oncoming traffic. Nobody but Dave is there to judge me when I disappear headfirst into bushes. Dave watches me progress from wobbly to smooth and straight – with zeal.

BONDING WITH
STRANGERS

I am often in agreement with Jean-Paul Sartre's idea that hell is other people, particularly other people on a sweaty, height-of-summer bus, or in a bar queue, or talking on speakerphone. But this makes it all the more pleasing when I find commonality and shared enjoyment with strangers.

One of the best examples of this is when watching sporting events. I cannot tell you the number of high-fives given and received with fellow Liverpool fans in random pubs – my best mates for ninety minutes, and without the lifelong lie of pretending to like their spouse. I have hugged people from every walk of life after a ball ricocheted off the crossbar and over the line in the final minute.

The bucolic version of this is the nod-and-smile that walkers exchange as they pass, wearing bucket hats and boots, fleeces with shorts: always an outfit for two seasons at once. We smile as if to say: 'Look at this! Nature! Not social media!' It's like sharing a secret, except it is hectares big and smells of pine and cow pats and not-work. I'm also what my friends call a 'mingler', by which I mean it is not uncommon for me to end up playing Scrabble with people from the next table over at the pub, exchanging niceties and numbers.

There is a beauty, too, in strangers coming together in collective annoyance. The mutual eye-roll on a delayed train or the group tut at jobsworth security guards. Conversely, there is the symbiotic ecstasy of a gig encore; the drunken, raucous laughter in the loos with people whose names you won't remember in the morning.

Despite the stranger danger we were warned of as children, strangers can represent safety, too: the women who don't know each other, but come together when a threatening situation unfolds; the men who step in, too; people, splashed on the front pages, who come to the aid of others in extreme danger or natural disasters.

It is said that a measure of a society is how it treats its most vulnerable. I think it can also be measured by how its strangers interact: how they intersect, rub along and share spaces, experiences and moods. From something as simple as a door held open, to the stranger who pulls you by the collar from the path of an oncoming lorry.

It might be going too far to say that heaven is other people, but I will never not love the interchanging of spirit, or the quasi-religious experiences that can be shared with someone you don't know from Adam.

TRAVELLING LIGHT

I have crossed borders with nothing but a rucksack on my back. Arrived in countries with one holdall, not a scrap more. One year, at midnight, I booked a plane ticket for 7 a.m. that same day from London to Glasgow, packed a bag barely heavier than the quotidian, and off I went. I have gone to Morocco and Egypt in similar circumstances.

Travelling is wonderful, but the downsides – with air travel in particular – are easy to acknowledge: the dragging of heavy suitcases (often with a wonky wheel or broken handle); the queuing; the waiting around for luggage – and the potential for it to be lost; the paying extra for, seemingly, everything. The poor sods rifling through their carefully folded underwear to find something of sufficient weight to remove, rather than pay an extortionate £40 surplus-baggage fee.

Smugness is not a quality to cultivate, but I can't tell you that it isn't immensely satisfying not to have to worry about all of the above when travelling light. It isn't always possible, of course – work trips, longer holidays – but when it is, it's perhaps the closest thing to feeling free. It's a twist on that hole-in-a-sack riddle: what can you pack that will make your bag light? Nothing.

I have travelled in the opposite situation, too. When I moved back to the UK after living in Russia, a huge, framed Klimt print I had bought in Moscow six months earlier had its own plane seat. (I didn't buy it its own seat, but the stewards were keen on protecting it.) It hangs in my flat to this day, but it was incredibly stressful, moving with everything I owned.

I often travel alone. It is good for the soul. All I need is: my passport; a good book or three; a playlist relevant to where one is going; a language app (if relevant); a rolling countryside view from a train window, or a pointillist expanse from a plane window; and possibly, depending on mood, an incredibly interesting seat partner from whom one learns new things.

Because how many pairs of jeans are you really going to wear? Why take weighty bottles of shampoo when every hotel, Airbnb, or couchsurfing host will have some? Not having much on the back means one's plans can always change on a whim, too. And, in my opinion, plans are made for changing.

BEING FED BY
FRIENDS

I used to be someone who ate just for fuel, as some people work only to earn money.

It's not that I disliked food: I've always been devoted to English breakfasts and Sunday roasts and obsessed with eggs in all forms; prone to finding immense comfort in jam and toast or going to an Italian restaurant and ordering masses of pasta followed by affogato.

It is just that I never saw eating as an event. I viewed it as a side course. Breakfast omelette with one eye on a book. Quick sandwich at my desk checking Twitter during lunch break. Balancing a dinner plate on a cushion watching Netflix. Meals weren't a chore, but I was not someone who planned ahead and got excited about them. I didn't savour food. I took it for granted.

Then more and more friends came into my life who adore food. They are loyal to some recipes and experiment with others, yet who are never snobbish or judgmental about the fact I occupy a highchair of ignorance when it comes to all things culinary. One pal has an array of pans hanging over her kitchen island, the names of many I couldn't tell you; pans that I am seemingly incapable of not headbutting. But this is not a column on how I learned to cook, even though I am slowly – as if on the lowest heat – making progress.

This is a column on how lovely it is to be cooked for. I used to find being cooked for stressful, for two reasons: I felt panicked by witnessing skills that highlighted my inadequacy; and I felt guilty and rude because I could not return this particular act of generosity. I haven't sung for my supper at dinner parties, exactly, but I have done a lot of insisting on washing up and bringing large bottles of booze.

The huge joy, I have discovered, in being cooked and baked for by people for whom food is an obsession – eating it, making it, thinking about it, writing about it, eating some more of it – but who above all prioritise those at their table, is that it is a transferable pleasure. I now enjoy cooking by proxy. It makes me happy to make my friends happy, and I have learned that enjoying the food someone else has cooked for me will do that.

Feeding someone is an act of love; a way of bestowing life – even if that life comes in the shape of Victoria sponge. Especially, in fact, if it comes in the shape of Victoria sponge. My mouth and heart are full.

THE TO-DONE LIST

I have never been great at to-do lists. To me, they are an exercise in torture: writing a list of all the things I will inevitably not get done; a document of imminent failure. In a gameshow host voice: 'Here's what you could have done!'

However, for many people, ticking items off a to-do list is the definition of a quotidian pleasure; mini mood-boosts, micro injections of achievement. It could be argued that getting smaller tasks done supplies the motivation for the more expansive changes one needs to make in life. (Though sometimes this is wishful thinking: remember buying a stationery set before the new school year – despite already owning all the items; as though new pencils would augur a change in attitude from 'class clown' to diligent student?)

I sigh at chores and errands. I hide from returning emails. I am not superb, basically, at life's admin. But I have developed a trick: to-done lists. Or at least that is what I am calling them, ungrammatical as it is.

The to-done list is the art of writing down all the things I have done. I get the same boost others do when completing something on their to-do list; it is just that, in adding something to a blank page, I am not reminded of all the things I have yet to do, uncrossed out.

In a move that perhaps is taking it that little bit too far, I have begun to keep my to-done lists in a giant Google doc. A cumulative record of what, if anything, I managed to accomplish that day. No contribution is too small. To give you a glimpse into the glamorous life I lead, previous entries have included such Gatsby-esque pleasures as 'Cancelled direct debit' and, a personal favourite, 'Gave away coathangers on Freecycle'. But, in general, these lists mean I can keep tabs on when my productivity is spiralling or feel smug when looking back at an efficient week.

If the list is bulky, I end the day more settled, and I suppose it is an act of that overused and sometimes queasy term 'self-care'. It is a way of feeling proud of oneself in bitesize. So, if you are in the market for a way to de-stress, to enjoy the little wins – and who isn't? – I suggest the to-done list. This weekend's column? Done. I will be adding it to the list.

CARING LESS

I don't want to be dishonest, so I'll say that in caring what people think about this column, I am perhaps denying myself the peace I've found in caring less. Because caring is often important and rewarding: I want to write a good column so that you enjoy reading it. I want to make sure my friends are OK. People who do not care, or lack empathy, are sociopaths.

But oh, good god, I care about so many things that should not matter. I am now thirty-two. For reasons too depressing to go into, I wasn't always sure I would see thirty. Lots of you will be older than I am, perhaps much older. I've always had friends in this bracket, so I cannot be fooled by talk of wisdom. I know that, whatever age, we never escape ourselves.

What I do know to be true, however, is the pleasure to be found in not bothering about certain things. Because of a clinically malfunctioning brain, I am probably less proficient at this than the average person, and always will be. Still, the older I get, the better I am at caring less.

You can see the signs of caring too much in the way teenagers often present themselves at swimming pools, how they fold in on themselves to hide their bodies. Or the way a tiny logo embroidered on a shirt takes on great importance. I am a people-pleaser, which I think of as a good thing, but I have discovered that some people will never be pleased. Or don't deserve to be.

It used to be that, if I thought someone peripheral disliked me (which is rare, obviously: I'm amazing), I would spend a lot of time ruminating instead of indulging in the appreciation of friends and colleagues and the happiness therein. Often it turned out that X didn't dislike me, sometimes the opposite; I had just unilaterally decided it.

It turns out that caring less – the cousin of letting go – brings a joyful release. It's like taking a bra off at the end of the day or letting a ridiculously large backpack drop to the floor.

As I say, I don't want to tell you this is something I have conquered because that would not be true and, I expect, never will be. But progress is a step towards contentment. Run without worrying about overtakers. Brunch wearing your comfortable joggers. Be bored by the film the critics are raving about. Who cares? Not me. And, hopefully, not you.

THE SMELL OF
WOOD

My grandfather had a shed. That isn't a boast. That would be like boasting that he had a cardigan. Or that he said that things were better in his day. Or never talked about the war. That would be like boasting about having had a grandad. But, oh man, I loved that shed. It was at the end of the garden, past the football goal I had set up, past the beds of flowers I trampled with a ball, and it smelt of wood. Glorious wood.

It was a workshop. Beyond the clanking of a triple lock on the door was a treasure trove of saws and nuts and bolts and screws and sanders and vices and chisels and bar clamps. Coils of wood shavings covered the floor. Tiny particles of ash hung in the sunlight shining through the little window. The air filled with a deep, fresh-cut scent. No wonder Jesus was a carpenter: the smell of wood is next to godliness.

I was reminded of all this when I passed a furniture shop last week and saw a man in overalls sanding down a table in a small courtyard. I never became any good at cutting wood or carving or sanding. I made a lot of 'door wedges', a lot of 'spare Jenga blocks'. But I was humoured enough to have a go, and isn't that one of the greatest gifts of grandparents?

I get my hit these days by walking in forests. Roaming around the north and south forests of Hampstead Heath in London, where there are more than 800 trees. Some of the oaks are estimated to be at least 500 years old. When I am back north, I go walking with a group of friends in the 2,400 acres of Delamere Forest, Cheshire, the largest forest in the county. It's packed with deciduous trees and evergreens. Different types of wood smell differently: the fresh smell of a maple rounders bat is not the same as a willow cricket bat. The smell of an Edwardian secondhand mahogany desk changing the aroma of a room is its own singular kind of pleasure, separate from the sweet, mossy scent of wet wood after a downpour.

Many people enjoy a good sniff of wood. Cedar is a popular ingredient in perfumes (I will always remember an episode of *The Apprentice* in which one team mistook cedarwood oil for the much more expensive sandalwood oil, blowing £700). And I don't know anybody who doesn't like the smell of Christmas trees or sitting rooms in National Trust properties. I'm not the only one who pines for pine, who goes weak for walnut.

EUROPEAN TOWN
SQUARES

I have favourite squares in Britain: Radcliffe Square in Oxford, dominated by its majestic camera; Millennium Square in Leeds; Trafalgar Square in London. Other favourites are much farther away: my breath was stolen by St Petersburg's Palace Square; I was bowled over by Cairo's Tahrir Square; charmed by Marrakech's Jemaa el-Fnaa.

But who does town squares best? Continental Europeans, of course. That's why we often describe squares by their Italian name: piazzas. I have special memories of Pariser Platz in Berlin and Livu Square in Riga. When those of us not from the continent think of our finest holiday moments, I would wager that tucking into lunch, sipping a coffee, nibbling ice-cream, people-watching or chatting with a companion, all while sitting al fresco at a piazza table, are up there with other delights such as lounging on a beach, going on long walks and haggling in markets.

As with so many of the great things in life, we have the Greeks to thank for coming up with the idea of a central meeting place: the agora. (Hence agoraphobia, the fear of public places.) Back then, poets and philosophers would meet to entertain and share ideas – because public squares consist of people enjoying each other's company. They serve as locations for municipal celebrations, the screening of sporting events and firework displays. (Of course, they can also serve as places of protest.)

So we must look after them. Whenever Venice's Piazza San Marco is flooded, the pictures of it underwater are devastating. I've visited San Marco three times, and each memory has a different flavour: family holiday; school trip; friends' getaway. But there's a balance between caregiving and overprotectiveness. I'm thinking of Rome, banning people from sitting on the Spanish Steps; this is a shame, especially for tourists, because watching the bustle of a community – and an unfamiliar one that speaks a different tongue – brings a special contentment and should never be banned.

I cannot wait, then, to be back sipping cool lemonade. Or watching a street performer, resoundingly applauded by a crowd. Admiring locals in high heels expertly traversing ancient cobbles. Chatting into the evening, shifting a chair to follow the last dapples of sun. Stopping for a nightcap on the leisurely walk back to the hotel, lights shining, like the EU stars, overhead.

TECH REPRIEVES

Something guaranteed to make my stomach lurch (aside from running out of teabags) is tech failure. Oh, it comes in many forms: the spinning beachball of doom on a Mac; the strangled, high-pitched beeps of a keyboard; the deep groan of a laptop shutting down for no apparent reason; and one time, a loud pop, flames, and an obliteration of the motherboard of my desktop. All of my data – years' worth – disappearing in a strong-smelling, smoky haze. Like magic: but dark, dark magic.

And that's just computers. In an absurd act of self-sabotage, I have also owned multiple iterations of iPhones for the past decade, despite the fact a third of them have given up on me – one day just switching off, never to switch back on. No amount of button-pressing combinations (the phone equivalent of CPR) brought them back. It is infuriating and devastating. There have been hot, hiccupping tears.

I've lost tens of thousands of photos, tens of thousands of words. In hindsight, I am sure, no, I know, some of them deserved to go. But, still. At the time, I mourned. I used to own so many USB sticks on lanyards that I resembled a prison officer with a multitude of keys. Somehow flash-drive errors followed me around. I bought external hard drives for backup, and they perished.

This was all before the advent of cloud storage, but a combination of scattiness and making masses of content means that I frequently run out – and then forget to buy more data. (At this point I should sheepishly mention that I worked as a tech journalist for two years.)

The heart-lifting opposite of tech failure is a tech miracle. That ecstatic transition from an open-mouthed, Munch-like suspended scream to a wide grateful grin at the reappearance of a lost doc, a sputtering reboot. I have punched the air.

Sometimes it's a joy undeserved. You don't know what happened, but it did, and that is all that matters. Other times, it is the reward of subjecting oneself to helpline hold music for forty-five minutes, or downloading patches or disk recovery software, or begging, on numerous forums, strangers for advice: someone, please, help. I am not sure which is the greater satisfaction; the spontaneous tech-redemption or the hard investigative graft paying off. Sometimes, as with simultaneous medical treatments, it isn't clear what truly made the difference. But who cares? All is not lost.

ABANDONING
A BOOK

I love reading books I hate. I used to hate it because I was one of those people who would force myself to finish a book, even if every turn of the page filled me with unmitigated dread. Even if each sentence made my brain wince. For some reason, I placed moral value on not giving up until I had reached the back cover.

I no longer do that. I learned that life is too short to indulge in things that do not give a great return on my energy, emotion or time. So really, you might say I enjoy tossing a book I am disliking across a room (though I'm not cavalier enough to do that: I just snap it shut in a decisive way). The relief of calling time on something one is not enjoying, and which is not enriching, brings a warmth and lightness.

But it's true that even before that moment of abandonment – during the actual reading of awfulness – some pleasure sneaks in. Perhaps it is a type of schadenfreude. I might think: 'Well, if writing as poor as this can be published and sell, I can't do much worse.' Maybe it's written by someone I know to be awful as a person and therefore I relish their subpar prose. What is great about bitching about a book is that it doesn't leave one with a sense of guilt. It is not an ad hominem attack. If I ask a friend whether they have read X and they reply that they hated it – and I did, too – that is the perfect base for a wonderful conversation.

Obviously, I love reading books where I am savouring every sentence. But the problem with being a writer and reading immensely pleasurable work is creeping feelings of inadequacy and envy, i.e., the opposite of the encouragement and fillip and unattractive competitive streak that the badly written books elicit.

There's an added bonus, too, one that I think of as altruistic but that you will now know is nothing of the sort. After I have dismissed a book, banished it from my hands, I will give it to charity. One time, when I was young and didn't really understand etiquette (or anything), I put a used toothbrush in a care package that churches collect and then send abroad. I know. Donating a crap book to a charity shop is the literary equivalent. If you have ever picked up a painful novel or some nonfiction drier than the Sahara, then I'm so sorry; I cannot promise I am not responsible. My advice? Toss it across the room.

PLAYING
BOARD GAMES

Monopoly, Scrabble, Trivial Pursuit, Operation, Mousetrap; when a man is bored of board games, he is bored of life. Playing with friends is so relaxing an activity, I can imagine even paid-up gangsters cracking open a few beers and getting the Connect 4 out. As wild teens who took a lot of drugs and frequently woke up with hangovers in bathtubs, my friends and I would still enjoy nights gathered around a coffee table playing Bananagrams. I recall, too, a tender moment during a school detention – one of those lax, end-of-term ones – when I taught a tough lad chess and he taught me draughts.

There are people who profess not to like board games, but I feel they have just not met the right game for them. Risk, for instance, has a legion of fans, but if I were an alien dropped into mid-play with no other board game experience, I, too, would think they were not for me. (No shade towards Risk-lovers: I just find political conflict and war depressing enough IRL. I'm much happier strapping a plastic bee on to my head and playing the nineties classic Bizzy Buzzy Bumbles.)

As a child, my family would make an annual visit to a beach house in Cumbria (six converted and connected railway carriages). In the evenings, games of Monopoly would be conducted with a view of high tide – as though the sea, too,

wanted to play. With an early bedtime, half-finished games would be put away overnight to be returned to the next evening. I cheated every time, stashing pink notes before recommencing. Nothing was said, but I am sure everyone knew.

Luckily, my family is small, and therefore games of charades were never played at Christmas, a routine I am told can turn stressful and sour. I was, however, often a sore loser. I have mellowed in this regard (although perhaps that is a result of playing with friends rather than relatives). Now, I think playing chess or Scrabble with one other person, in concentrated but comfortable silence, is an understated sign of love.

If I may, I would like to touch on card games. Poker I am bad at because I cannot hold my emotions in, ever. But Ring of Fire and the quite iconic Shithead – both of which involve alcohol as a key participant – make for raucous bonding. That said, when I attempted to introduce the former to pals in Russia, they looked perplexed and said: 'I do not understand. Why would you need an excuse to drink?'

HANDWRITTEN
LETTERS

I used to have a pen pal, as a pre-teen. She lived in Spain. We would write to each other on embossed paper, weighed down with elaborate stickers.

The letters smelled of perfume or sweets. They came in the most exciting envelopes I have ever seen. Red-and-blue borders. A little logo of a plane and AIR MAIL or PAR AVION on them.

The men in the Spanish stamps had impressive beards. Usually there would be multiple paper stamps and then circles of ink on top of those; a busy little corner of navigation. The envelopes from my pen pal were cream, the ones I bought from my local post office were a pale blue, the same shade as my short-sleeved school shirts.

Nothing exciting comes through my letterbox now. There is nothing with that inky, intimate thrill. Bills (despite the fact that I long ago requested email statements only), not only my own, but those for the tenants before me, and the ones before them. Lucky me! Leaflets for kebab shops, though I am vegetarian. Sometimes folded sheets from estate agents, which sycamore down to the tiled hall, inquiring as to whether I want to sell my flat which is not, in fact, my flat. Hospital reminders, which mostly arrive after the date of the appointment, PRIVATE AND CONFIDENTIAL written on the envelope.

The things I am fortunate to receive, both expected and unexpected, are books – secondhand ones I have ordered greedily online, but also the surprise thud of proof copies that publishers send me for review.

Occasionally a love interest will send me notes, written in beautifully cursive script – as is proper – with small gifts enclosed. A healing crystal, once, after I had admitted knowing nothing about such things. Postcards, wittily annotated. But sifting through a pile of letters and recognising familiar handwriting is a now an all-too-rare thrill.

It's not that I don't appreciate modern communication. WhatsApp banter and voice memos are fun. Phone calls I enjoy more and more. But text, email and chat windows do not have the personality of looping words or near-indecipherable scrawls. My father used to write me absurdly long letters – polemics way too complex for an eight-year-old to parse – but at the end, he would tape a few strands of the dog's hair and always signed off with a drawing of a paw. I looked forward to these letters so much.

Anyway, the address of Faber's office can be found on their website. Just saying.

A CLEAN HOME

There are many variations on the maxim 'tidy desk, tidy mind'. And, though I am somewhat bastardising Newton's third law of motion here, an untidy desk should therefore equal an untidy mind. While I am not sure of the causal relationship, I definitely have both of those.

To avoid becoming a local newspaper story of a hoarder, photographed surrounded by copies of the same local newspaper with previous stories of hoarders – a sort of recurring Droste effect of hoarders, if you will – I practise tidiness. I find it very boring and, though we all find many things boring, I actually take medication for it. My brain never has waves, but storms. So, things that bore me I find almost impossible to do. Setting up a direct debit is one of the most difficult things in the world for me, although it takes approximately four minutes and can mean the difference between receiving a court summons and not.

I used to kick the idea of tidying under the bed; shove it to the back of the wardrobe. Shunt it into another room. Throw a blanket over it. But while I am not yet fully reformed, then I am reforming. Because I have learned that a clean and tidy home is one of the most happy-making things. It is still pleasing if someone else is responsible (a professional cleaner, a partner, etc), but actually doing the graft and then living with – in the best sense – the result, is a feeling I love. I feel genuine pride when a drawer can slide smoothly into my desk rather than jamming, overstuffed with papers. Or when I know I am sitting on my sofa, minus 9,000 receipts and corners of Doritos between the cushions.

I don't understand how cleaning has become a popular genre on Instagram, or Mrs Hinch a bestselling phenomenon, but I have watched certain stain-removal tutorials on YouTube. There are entire forums full of tricks on how to clean windows without streaks, passed down through generations.

I still find cleaning dull, but once I get into it, at least I am fully focused on how fragrant the finish will be. Shakespeare was correct: all that glisters is not gold. But I'm content if it's just my chrome tap.

The process itself does have some advantages: doing things with one's hands is a great distraction. I simply don't have the capacity to stress about a pandemic, or Donald Trump possibly winning a second term as president, when I'm cleaning in between floorboards with a cotton bud. And there's a sentence I never thought I'd write – in every sense.

FAVOURITE SONGS
ON SHUFFLE

Most people have favourite songs and the majority of the time, we hear them by our own hand. For the most part, I don't agree with the sentiment that one can play a loved song too much and ruin it. I have a rapacious attitude to things I take great pleasure in, and though we can fall out of love with people, places and things, it is rare for me to get sick of a song. (Conversely, I do believe in the power of the grower.)

Songs become favourites for various reasons. Perhaps a track is tied to a memory. Sometimes it is the craft of a near-perfect work. Maybe it is impossible not to dance to. People have favourites that might not induce happiness but provide some other emotional release. It's possible the lyrics are extremely relatable. Frequently, it is a combination.

With the advent of new technologies, many of us listen to music in a medium that would have been unrecognisable not long ago. There is a healthier market for records than one might expect, due to a sort of faux nostalgia from young people who were not around for their heyday. MiniDiscs (lol) and the cracked jewel cases of CDs are, for most of us, no more. Streaming rules; I am not sure Gen Z would understand 'MP3'.

But the feature that has transformed us most as listeners is shuffle. A favourite track coming up on shuffle is the roulette ball landing on the correct number – but as though someone else had chosen it for you. Shuffle is the equivalent of a DJ dropping a banger. I really don't want to say that people 'throw their hands in the air like they just don't care', but, well, they do. Now we can have that similar unexpected joy via earbuds on the commute to work, or when sweating on a treadmill, providing an extra kick of energy.

Sometimes a good shuffle isn't as random as it might seem: algorithms pick up on the songs we appreciate most and, like a dog being trained, the shuffle alters its behaviour accordingly. It isn't that a song's sudden hello hasn't thrown me into the past and elicited stealthy tears (I don't want to talk about it), or a song I hate hasn't sneaked its way in when I'm listening to a suggested playlist.

Turning on shuffle is worth the risk: to hear the opening thrum of a classic that makes the heart beat faster, your smile grow wider and a shiver run down the spine.

BUMPING INTO
FRIENDS

Few would deny the awkwardness of bumping into someone you'd rather not. Not even, necessarily, somebody you
dislike: perhaps it's a colleague on the bus, and you are tired.
Or it's a friend of a friend; likable but loquacious. It's an ex.
Oh god, it's an ex.

But the discomfort of hoping your neighbour from four
years ago doesn't notice you in a doctor's waiting room can
be matched only by the pleasure of a serendipitous meeting
of an old acquaintance walking her dog or – this happened to
me – spotting a school friend, by chance, on the other side of
the world.

These days we have more means of communication than
ever. And yet, often it can feel as though we are living
through a time of scant true connection. We are always
in touch. But that's it, really – just a touch. A grazing of
interrelation. A cycle of hi-and-bye. Read receipts, but not
necessarily a taking-in of information.

What a joy, what a bonus, to run into someone one hasn't
seen in an age. Someone with whom drinks have had to be
rearranged and postponed, seemingly in perpetuity. It's like
finding a fiver, except you know the person on the note.

I love people. I do. (Not all of them. Some of those who

sit on green benches at the moment, in particular, I would be less keen to share a lift with.) But there are many people in my life with whom I am thrilled to share encounters: core friends, or those on the periphery. And when it is people I haven't seen in a while, whom I regret falling out of contact with – well, it's almost a miracle. The universe gift-wrapping a moment.

Before mobile phones, even arranged meet-ups were a kind of bumping into people. Meet in this place, at this time. Scanning the crowds outside the cinema or packed bar, at 1 p.m. That brief anticipation of seeking recognition rather than a text reading: Here.

Sometimes, I lie awake at night and wonder where certain people are at that exact time. My first love. The clan of amazing people I lived with when I was abroad, who took me in and fed me pelmeni. What are the chances of suddenly being in the same location, at the same strike of the clock?

The distant cousin of the unplanned meet is realising that you and another will be in nearby places at similar times and deciding to slightly alter itineraries to meet in the middle. But it's even better meeting in the middle when neither of you had any idea it was the middle. See you soon. Hopefully.

A SHIMMERING
REFLECTION

Humans are both vain and insecure; in fact, two sides of the same coin. Perhaps because, too often, for me the latter outweighs the former, I don't love looking into mirrors. I do, however, love reflections.

Some are shimmering, dancing: the light that bounces from lido water as one cuts through it; the way a sea, in the distance, is studded with diamonds. At home, clearing out an old chest, I found a miniature mirrorball. I have no idea where it came from, but as I placed it on the floor, intending to discard it later, the sun streamed through my window and threw bright yellow squares all across the room: the walls, the ceilings, the fireplace. I kept the mirrorball there. Every time it is sunny, the room is lit up. It is stunningly beautiful and I appreciate it each time.

I have written a whole other piece about riding the night bus as, if not a cure for depression and insomnia, then a distraction, and to smuggle in some human contact in the form of the brief interaction with the driver. When the windows are black in the small hours of the morning, it is possible to see out of both sides of the bus at the same time; for neon signs that I have never noticed in daylight to catch my attention even if I am looking elsewhere. It's dark, yet you see more.

Occasionally reflections are not so benign. I have a memory that makes me laugh out loud and, at the same time, burn with shame. About to turn the corner to meet a friend on a windswept day, I quickly crouched down to check my reflection in a car window – before realising someone was in the car, now looking askance at my looming face. This happened to a friend, too, when she was appraising her outfit in what she thought was an empty shop front, only to have a builder wave at her.

The thing about reflections is that, often, the clue is in the name. If I am looking at the surface of a lake, say, I often find myself in deep thought or concentration on the past, or the future, or all time in between. I'm not sure, but I get the feeling I am not unique in this. There is something captivating about this trick of light and science. Something transcendent.

Except for having to close the curtains to watch a television or laptop. That's not transcendent. On reflection, that's just annoying.

A RUNNING HIGH

It's rare that someone looks forward to exercise all of the time – even if one enjoys playing sports (as I do) or can barely remember the direct route home from the office because they always stop off at the gym first. Even professional athletes talk of wanting to stay in bed and skip training.

I used to do what I call – many apologies – 'gym 'n' swim', which is what you'd imagine. I never did one without the other, because the opportunity to cool down in the water after time on the treadmill or bike – and the strenuous activity of watching others lift weights – was too inviting. Even if my shoulders ached with fatigue and I only did a few laps, I felt so good afterwards. I don't like to write that because it will annoy plenty of people, just as when runners told me about the 'high' that running gave them, while it gave me the sensation that my lungs were made of concrete. What is this high, I wanted to counter. Where does it hide? But a couple of friends wrote books about it, and it felt rude not to give it a go.

I am still not good at running, which is slightly dispiriting to admit. But when I crossed my first 5k finishing line after taking it up again, I felt elated. A short distance, yes, but it's a hard slog when you feel sick for the duration. It was almost as though the redder my face, the happier I felt.

I could talk about endorphins here, but I am not going to because people talk about endorphins too much. I want to describe the effect without the science: which is the appreciation and wonder of the body. Not the shape or size or extent of its ability, but rather reaching its full potential – or heading that way – whatever its limitations. Starting to move it in any significant way, and regularly, is the hardest part, and I admit that I am, at present, at the point of having to restart. But I know it will be worth it; that – conversely – after working my legs until they're heavy, I will have a spring in my step. Team sports add an element of social pleasure and the reward of potential triumph.

No doubt there are people sitting at home with icepacks pressed to strained glutes, or elbows in slings, who are are thinking 'never again'. But I am sure they will go back, like besotted lovers, to the thrill of a pumping heart. Or – fine, I'll say it – those glorious endorphins.

AN OPEN FIRE

I almost die every time I see the final scene of *Call Me by Your Name* (three times and counting): it's a four-minute fixed camera shot in which the lead character sits in front of a crackling fireplace with tears brimming but not quite escaping, a lip bitten as he silently contemplates his first, and lost, love. Maybe I have made it sound cheesy; it isn't.

This scene would not have worked if, say, it had been the same character staring forlornly out of a window, or stroking a battered photograph kept in a wallet. Fires can be pure poetry.

Each year, when I head north to the family house for Christmas and New Year, the thing I look forward to most is stretching out in front of the fire alongside the cat; his belly hot to the touch, his chin turned upwards. In the curves of the brass fender, the Christmas tree lights reflect in blurs.

Like most writers, I have zero practical skills. Except for one: I can lay and light a fire. This comes from observing my mother doing origami with old newspaper pages, cross-hatching logs and kindling, and picking up and setting down efficiently sized bits of coal as though they were priceless gems, with a set of delicate tongs.

One January a few years ago, my then girlfriend and I rented a cottage by the seaside in Deal, Kent. While my partner went to collect a food order, I rolled up my sleeves and got to work on the fireplace. When she returned, sodden from the rain and carrying Tupperware filled with chicken tikka masala, the flames were bold red and orange and rippling. We ate, played Scrabble and scratched her terrier under its ears.

I now live in a flat that has fireplaces in two rooms, and I am looking up the telephone numbers of chimney sweeps. There is a local firm that has been run by the same family since 1860. The fireplaces are beautiful things: just one can add 5 per cent to the value of a home. There is a downside, however, and that is the environmental impact. At its most extreme: the pea-souper smog of 1952, which led to the Clean Air Act. Real fires, then, are recommended in moderation.

But fake ones that have to be plugged in and switched on won't do, either. Or, even worse, digital fires on television screens. I don't have the same objection to wallpaper of woodlands or plants but, to paraphrase John Waters, if you go home with somebody and they have a DVD of a home fire, don't fuck them. Home is where the hearth is.

CANCELLED PLANS

Someone once told me that when you are first invited to something, before committing to it for a future date, you should ask yourself if you would want to do it that same day. I often find this is good advice. If you would dread it in three hours' time, you are likely to dread it in three weeks' time.

All too often, however, we say yes to things we have no or limited interest in; networking events; reunions; 'enriching' experiences. Or perhaps there are things you want to do – meeting up with friends; theatre trips – but, on the day, it is raining, or you are exhausted, or there's a television show you are addicted to and cannot wait to finish. In any case, the important factor here is: you'd rather not go.

The act of cancellation looms. Do you lie? 'I'm afraid something has come up' (i.e. being curled up on the sofa has come up). Do you convince yourself the head cold you have is a much more serious ailment? Are you honest, but feel guilty and flaky? It's an anxiety-inducing conundrum. Nobody wants to let a person down. But also: nobody wants to travel fifty minutes across three boroughs to go to a baby shower.

This is where, if luck is on your side, a truly glorious reprieve is granted: the thing you do not want to do is cancelled. It is the social-life equivalent of gearing up to dump a partner only for them to get in first. I have genuinely felt a thrill when receiving a text full of apologies from a friend who can't make a one-on-one rendezvous when I have been sitting at home trying to gee myself up to head out again for the evening. (Nothing to do with their company; everything to do with laziness or malaise.) An added bonus of being cancelled on when you secretly welcome it is you get to look extremely magnanimous in response. (Though perhaps you are honest in your shared relief. I have admitted to it before to soothe guilt-ridden friends.)

The flipside is that it sucks to be cancelled on when you are looking forward to something. An afternoon with an old friend and a new exhibition. Or a football match or festival rained off. But oh, what a relief when a dull dinner party at which people talk about the colours of their school ties is taken off the table.

It's a lovely thing, escape – even more so when it's somebody else lifting the fence.

GOING TO THE
CINEMA ALONE

When I was a kid, if I spotted someone alone at the cinema I would label them a sad sack. I am ashamed to admit this, but I would peg them as a loser; or I would feel sorry for them, because I assumed they had no friends.

I wonder if teenagers think this of me, now that I go to the cinema alone more frequently than with company. While I enjoy going with a pal, to dissect a film or performance afterwards, perhaps it is even more of a pleasure to assess it in one's own head, in solitude – turning it over in the mind, forming an opinion untainted by conversation.

It also means that I am free to react like a weirdo as the end credits roll, should I need to. Did I cry uncontrollably at the end of *Manchester by the Sea*? No comment. Did I subtly air drum after seeing *Whiplash*? I simply couldn't tell you. I distinctly remember, when resident at a non-secure mental health facility, popping to the nearest cinema one evening to see *The Big Short*, and feeling something for the first time in weeks, wheeling away in pleasure, thinking that maybe – just maybe – I was getting better.

I am entirely happy in my own company; this extends to eating alone or travelling by myself. I affectionately call a colleague and good friend Walk Me to Biology, because she won't go to places alone, like the girls in school who seemed incapable of making their way to class without an escort.

Please don't misunderstand me – I have no qualms whatsoever about bringing a friend or partner to the flicks. (Unless they are a talker, then – no. I am sure many friendships have been severed when someone frequently asks at the beginnings of films, 'What is happening?', when the point of a film is that one finds out.)

It is important to me, with all art (in fact, with everything) to form my own opinions before opening up to the input, potentially mind-changing, of others. I will never read reviews of films before watching them. I prefer to gain just a gist – usually by star ratings – of whether something is worth going to see.

Yes: better to go alone. Especially when I get the popcorn all to myself.

TRAINERS

Three years ago, I became sober for a year – despite the best efforts and influence of a good friend and esteemed colleague who shall remain nameless (Zoe Williams). There were a lot of things I noticed about going from someone who rocked into the office, mossy-tongued and permanently hungover, to booze-free. The most obvious three were: time; money; energy. All of these beneficial changes – I had more of all of them – contributed to two things I suddenly became enamoured with, having shown little interest in them before. Those things are techno music (previously my idea of please god, no) and trainers.

While friends spent their mornings under duvets in the foetal position, I was up if not quite with the larks, then early enough to plan my day, spread out ahead of me like a map. I started to walk around the city, discovering tiny side streets the width of a horse-drawn carriage. This satisfied my increased time and energy (as did the new love of techno music), and the money I previously directed to my liver found a new home on the soles of my feet.

I'm not quite into the territory of calling trainers 'sneakers' in the manner of a US pretender, but since my enlightenment I have been known to call them kicks. In the north and in

Scotland, we call them trabs. Suddenly, I found myself filing copy about New Balance's position on the Trans-Pacific Partnership. New Balance is now one of my favourite brands, the more garish, I'm afraid, the better. I have a luminous turquoise-and-orange pair. Bright purple. Shocking pink. Neon green and grey. I see a lush pair of Nikes in a shop, consider buying them, then just do it. I now pronounce Nike with the 'ee' sound at the end, and Adidas with the stress on the first syllable. One learns the language.

People walk on air if they are in love, but also if they are wearing Nike Airs. Red Bull gives you wings; so do Jeremy Scott's limited editions. Fresh white Converse hi-tops are as much a wardrobe staple as a crisp, white shirt. I pick up bargains in charity shops, discount outlets, online and in the stores that spend 52 weeks of the year apparently closing down, but never do. I smile at kids in flashing pumps and respect the office-allowable, semi-professionalism of the Dunlop tennis shoe.

It might seem silly – frivolous, even – to have taken up trainers as a hobby. But as I would say to my mother when she chastises me for anything: at least it's not hard drugs. I am yet to reach the dizzy heights of an MTV Cribs walk-in-wardrobe. There's also this key advantage: now that I am drinking again (in moderation, guys!), trainer-shod, I am much less likely to fall over after one too many. The walk home is a doddle.

CHANGING
YOUR MIND

We crucify politicians for their U-turns and often it is justified. Flipflops, however, are rather different from the utter chaos we've seen in the last few years, where it would be more accurate to say government policy is under the influence of centrifugal force. Not so much about-turns but a general vortex of mess.

As easy as it is to slag off politicians and public figures (and I do my fair share), it is a mark of intelligence and good character to be able to have one's mind changed. I don't mean shifting opinions for individual gain; watching for whichever way the wind blows, then reneging on a previous position for self-preservation or popularity. I am talking about listening to a cogent argument, and sincerely adjusting one's outlook.

In school and universities, students practise this art through mooting competitions in borrowed courtrooms and debating clubs, but in the outside world we increasingly seem to have lost the ability to communicate our disagreements in good faith. Social media is a huge part of this. It is easier to rant and rave behind a screen than it is to behave similarly face to face. In lockdown, one of the things I missed most was sitting with friends in the pub and sharing our takes on current affairs or, say, the pattern of one of our shirts.

One of the buzz phrases with most traction in our current times is 'culture wars'. I dislike this term for a number of reasons. The first is that much of this 'war' is quite simply people fighting against bigotry versus bigots. Black Lives Matter isn't a debate. The second is that many of these 'wars' are concocted by agents who seek to benefit from keeping people engaged and divided. Our outrage is being monetised.

All of this is grim, which is why sensible discussion is such a pleasure. A change in conviction isn't necessarily indicative of fair-weather flimsiness. If a government department realises, 'Oh, actually, that might be better', then I'm all for it, as long as it is done in a way that is honest, not hypocritical. If I read a book and it alters my view of things, or educates me about other perspectives, that is time well spent. I have come to enjoy TV shows friends told me not to give up on; I like being dragged to an exhibition of an artist I didn't care for and later having to admit it was good. Being able to change one's mind, then, is a positive. But I am happy to consider dissent.

BROWSING
PROPERTY WEBSITES

According to Alexa, the most visited websites are those you would expect: Google, YouTube, Facebook, Amazon. But I know I am part of a dedicated group of people who spend a significant amount of time on the internet browsing property websites. This is not because I am an investor (cue hysterical laughter), or that I am buying a house. This is pure escapism.

Sites such as Rightmove, Modern House and Purple Bricks are my weakness; I'm afraid I have a passionate dislike of estate agents – because fool me once, shame on you; fool me ninety times and I will despise you for life – and a key bonus of escapist browsing is not having to deal with them. The properties I am looking at are £4-million townhouses in London, or vast open-plan warehouses in Glasgow, or cute bungalows in Pembrokeshire. I can also pass hours on WowHaus, which advertises places to stay. Recently, I have branched out into stalking lofts in New York and Berlin walk-ups on Google Street View.

My obsession pre-dates the internet. Whenever I was in a doctor's waiting room, I would dive into the dog-eared copies of *Country Life*, and even though I was sixteen with less than £100 in an ISA, would take in the Knight Frank manor houses for sale (two tennis courts, stables, a lake). Despite my later realisation that agents are essentially awful, I wanted to be one as a kid. I even made promotional brochures for my nonexistent agency. I played life-simulation videogame *The Sims* just to build the houses and I worked out a way to game it, so that I could add basements and double-height ceilings.

A significant factor when it comes to the homes that make me swoon is tiles. But so are chunky beams, and stained-glass windows in church conversions. I refuse to be shamed for spotting online that one of the pastel-coloured houses on my dream street has come on to the market, and then altering my route to work to walk by it, like a pining lover.

Lustily daydreaming after design works as a pressure release, a plaster of aesthetics on the wound of news. I suppose one might argue that downloading PDFs of the properties – as if I were actually going to put in an offer on Toddington Manor before Damien Hirst bought it (shut up) – might be taking it too far. But you must excuse me: I have a video tour of a Barbican penthouse to enjoy.

CEMETERIES

It sounds a little strange, I know, to say that cemeteries can be pleasurable places. You wouldn't think so, what with all the signposted mortality; everywhere you turn, a grey and mossy reminder of death; the shadow of the scythe. But it's the stillness, the respectful hush that I appreciate.

It's not a lofty silence. The sort found in a museum, predicated on intellect (or a performance of). It's not the tense, taut silence of an exam. The silence in a cemetery is a carefully weighted amalgam of love and reflection, and many more emotions besides. Not all easy, obviously, but part of the human experience.

My favourite cemetery is Highgate in London. People tend to focus on the famous and notable buried there. There is an entrance fee and a map. There is a tour. If you're interested in seeing a giant sculpted Karl Marx head, then Highgate is the one to visit. It is the final resting place of George Eliot and George Michael. It's fascinating to see the end points of such luminous lives, which is why the equally star-studded Père Lachaise in Paris seems to cameo in every film shot in the city.

It's the denser part of Highgate I like best, where the green grows thick and the stones are partly obscured. There is no death without life, and cemeteries are a rich source of tiny biographies: unheard-of occupations and conditions; an eyebrow-raising number of wives, or children, or both. The tragedy in dates too close together, evoking Hemingway's baby shoes, never worn. At Thiepval War Memorial to the Missing of the Somme a few years ago, I stood among row upon row of graves of boys the same age as I was then.

My favourite grave in Highgate? A tiny, unimposing stone belonging to one Fanny Toy. There is scant information about Fanny Toy's life, but her name is enough.

Often, the landscaping in cemeteries equals that of the best parks, and there is aesthetic joy to be found in certain memorials. In Highgate, the artist Patrick Caulfield has a wonderful, pop art inspired headstone. Some inscriptions make me laugh. The sassiest I've heard is Jesse James's (on the wish of his mother): 'Murdered by a traitor and coward whose name is not worthy to appear here.'

There is one other reason I can happily sit quietly in a cemetery on a sunny day at the end of a walk. And that is gratitude: I will admit that I have come close to death, and it is because I have sought it out. Cemeteries are not just the residencies of the dead, but places that reiterate the gift in living.

TILES

There is an Instagram account called @IHaveThisThing-WithFloors. I also have a thing with floors and so, apparently, do more than 830,000 other people. This account is the antidote to the snaps that smug holidayers take of their feet on beaches, sand spilling over their toes. Smug feet all look the same and sand is beige. But: I have this thing with floors. Specifically, with tiles and flagstones.

Some of my recent favourites that fellow floor enthusiasts have posted on the app include a fuchsia baroque floor; a multi-coloured ikat design; a tiled seascape decorating an indoor pool. In my flat, which is on the ground floor of a converted Victorian terrace, the traditional brown, blue, white mosaic diamond tiles of that period seep under the door from the main hallway. Every time I come home, I admire them. Well, I feed my cat, make a cup of tea and then I admire them.

Public loos – the few remaining – might not come top of most people's list of admiration, but oh my god: the tiles! Floors and walls. The riches! Not far from where I live, there are well-maintained public toilets where the monochrome check floor is offset by deep green, sheening walls. There is a grade II-listed pub down the road. Formerly a hotel that opened in 1899 and cost a then-extravagant £30,000, it is in the French renaissance style and has a treat of a bathroom: white tiled floors with splashes of red, yellow, and blue – like Mondrian, but if Mondrian had gone a bit Jackson Pollock. Mondrian if Mondrian had been drinking in the pub.

There are the tiles that look like Magic Eye paintings or the bright, geometric tiling in bars with overpriced cocktails and dim light. The fan designs of hotel lobbies and old theatres. The burgundy tiles of the Marrakech souks. The ornate teal-and-gold tiling in Turkish bathhouses. The cold, crumbling floors of Russian dachas that babushkas pad across to make evening chai. The country kitchens with an Aga and a perfect terracotta floor. The basic designs of monasteries. Or the ostentatious 1920s art deco designs underfoot in California, bursting with extravagant shapes and the promise of parties. Salvage yards and eBay listings feed my passion.

Tiled floors, the ceramic sort at least, have been a thing for thousands of years. The Egyptians enjoyed a glass tile. But it's the Industrial Revolution I have to thank for the boom in the type I have in my flat, when the potters of Victorian England were widespread and inexpensive. (Wealthier households went for the handpainted Arts and Crafts option: think William Morris.) The mark of respect for a truly great tile is to walk all over it. Yes, I most definitely have a thing with floors.

A TRIP TO THE
HAIRDRESSER'S

There was a time when I went years without visiting a hair-dresser. I know. But I found sitting bang in front of a starkly lit mirror faintly terrifying and so did my best to avoid it. Nobody enjoys confronting cavernous pores or realising that while you may think you are Galadriel, up close the vibe is more Gollum. There is also no silence I can leave unfilled; the stress of com-ing up with something witty or interesting to say left me in danger of losing hair, rather than having it improved.

I wish I could be one of those people who nails going to the hairdresser: saying nothing for four hours; flicking through *Vogue*, drooling over unaffordable clothes; relaxing into a head massage. Incidentally, who are the people who say no to the head massage? Would they refuse an oxygen mask on a plane?

It didn't help that as a child I was a committed tomboy and found anywhere with bottles of nail varnish overwhelming. My idea of dressing 'fancy' was wearing a darker shade of tracksuit. By the time that changed, I was firmly into home-dyes and cuts. I didn't think I was 'good' at going to the hairdresser's and so, like maths and cooking, I avoided it.

But then my sister gave me a haircut. Have you seen *I Know What You Did Last Summer*? Remember that bit where Sarah Michelle Gellar wakes up to find her hair has been hacked off overnight with a fishhook? I do. I lived it. Except I was awake throughout.

I was forced back to a salon and, in truth, my sister did me a favour, because this was my first meeting with my now regular hairdresser and colourist. While not qualified counsellors, they could legitimately whack an approximation of those skills on to their CVs. They also do a great line in bitching about Brexit.

I still do not appreciate the ridiculous amount of time it takes to colour a head of hair. It is still eye-wateringly expensive, but a cut and colour can perform miracles for mood. It's the aftermath: the unfathomable silkiness and the divine smell, the closeness to the temples, or the jaw, or the shoulder. But it's also the hypnotic snip-snip-snipping and the somnolent buzz of the razor. It's stepping back on to the street like a refurbished version of yourself. Not quite new, but newer. You, plus.

THE SEA

Give me all of the seas. The still teal around silver-beached islands, where the far-out horizon is a thin line of barely perceptible colour change. A Rothko. Give me the choppy waters of a Turner, peaks of spittle-white masquerading as icebergs. I want the deep navy with the surface wobble of jelly; or the entirely transparent water that laps at the shore, transforming my normal-sized feet into milky giants.

Give me all of the seas and let me swim in them. Cold water under December clouds that turns me Christmas-red when wading back out, feeling as though I could take on the world – and have just taken on a part of it, in fact. Floating on my back, in warm water, in a hot country, dunking my head to wash away sweat. Swivelling gently around for the fun of it, like a kebab.

For swimmers, each opportunity has its draw. I rather like the chlorine smell of indoor pools, the sounds echoing off the walls. The bored-looking parents sitting with their phones on the benches, half-returning the waves of kids with blue-and-white sponge floats. I enjoy the community spirit of outdoor lidos, seeing the same old faces. I have given the ducks in swimmable ponds names.

As trivia board games will tell us, 70 per cent of the Earth's surface is water and, of that, 97 per cent is the ocean. Every time we tiptoe towards it, bodies heavy with the added weight of wet sand, or picking out the easiest route via pebbles, and plunge in, we become part of its ecosystem.

We can see the fish flit back and forth, and jellyfish, which I am scared of, thanks to a documentary I once saw about the sting of the Portuguese man o' war (I mean, seriously, the name alone). But, for the most part, the only things that distract me – briefly – from the pleasures of the sea are slippery, mossy rocks, and seaweed pulling my ankles into an embrace.

Paddling, snorkelling, swimming, splashing: it is, without wanting to sound mawkish, a real gift, the sea. The 'locked' part of landlocked countries seems to speak to this. 'Locked' – a lack of the freedom of the ocean – seems appropriate, rather than, say, 'sea-less', which sounds neutral.

One time, as a teen, in that awkward stage of not realising everyone is too concerned with their own bodies to pay even a second's attention to yours, I went on a beach holiday and not once did I get in the sea. I think of that now, and I want to chuck past-me in: let the healing salt work its magic, wash it all away.

BLACK AND WHITE
PHOTOGRAPHS

Until the early 1980s, the revered photo agency Magnum did not allow members who shot exclusively in colour. Colour photographers were, if you like, the photographic equivalent of Dylan Going Electric.

A very many of my favourite photographers shoot – or shot – in glorious, highly saturated colour. Think of the pop of William Eggleston, or Martin Parr's exquisite capturing of the absurdism of British everyday life. But there is a unique quality to monochrome photographs. Monochrome photographs allow us to notice and focus upon things undistracted by colour. (Although, sidenote, there is a type of colour blindness, achromatopsia, in which individuals see only in shades of black and white.)

The body language of those in Diane Arbus's portraits – often strangers stumbled upon in Central Park. The attention to shadows and patterns of light by Alexander Rodchenko, for instance. Perhaps one of the most instantly recognisable black and white photographs is the sun pouring through the windows of Grand Central Station, as if the banks of a river of light had burst. (By Hal Morey.) The shapes of streets caught so viscerally by Henri Cartier-Bresson. The grooves of Samuel Beckett's face, deep as trenches in war, shot by the incredible

Jane Bown and now hanging in the National Portrait Gallery would not have had the same effect in colour. The visceral energy of Gordon Parks's civil rights photography.

The now much maligned Athena posters from the 1990s still hold affection and a kitsch place in pop culture. Though there are plenty of popular black and white prints which I'd happily send to the shredder for eternity (the one of the women in white vest tops and knickers kissing on a bed is supposed to be sexy but to me has strong vibes of falling asleep after a bath). There is also an epidemic of pics on Instagram with HDR whacked up and put through sepia filters.

The truth is, though, that while black and white photographs are often thought of as quieter that those in colour, they can be equally, if not more, powerful. (Parr actually started his career in black and white.) I hope – and am quietly confident in the matter – that black and white photography will continue to hold its own amongst canary yellows and lime greens and hot pinks.

HOUSE PARTIES

Who knows, in this time of compartmentalised living, when the house party will return? That incongruous mix of debauchery and a kitchenette. Queues for the bathroom as long as those for Michelin-starred restaurants. Sinks filled with ice and beers. Half-crushed paper cups on windowsills. For some reason, always liquorice-flavoured rollies.

House parties are wonderful because 90 per cent of the time they overdeliver. Usually, one dreads them – and then you're faced with excitable chat between people who are dear to you and those who are not; but, who knows, may become so.

I have run the gamut of house parties. Ones with caterers carrying trays of canapés, and ones where the carpet seems to have become an accepted ashtray. Ones in which the make-shift cloakroom in the bedroom includes furs and Burberry trenchcoats, and others where vintage shell-suit jackets jostle together in a burst of colour.

The most famous house party in culture must be Jay Gatsby's. A bacchanalian night, where the champagne and dresses flow gold, and no expense is spared. A riot of hedon-istic, epicurean delight – but ultimately very shallow, AKA my dream evening.

House parties do not tend to have a beginning, a middle and an end. They are shapeshifters; they are multidirectional. There is dancing to LCD Soundsystem, on the wooden floor of a sitting room, bottles precariously perched on a mantelpiece. There is a sidebar conversation in a conservatory. Politics maybe, but more likely gossip. Or gossip about people in politics. People with wide eyes and chewed lips who offer to share illicit goods. In a spare room, there is snogging.

Because the house party takes us back to our youth. I've said many times, 'I'm too old for house parties,' but the house party is never too old for you. It is the true members' club; a gate jamming on uneven flagstones is much better than a velvet rope.

The host, who you know and like, or the person who brings you, who you know and like, means that there is a high probability people at the party will be good ones. Fun ones. With interesting conversation and sharp wit. Or just really attractive.

My favourite house party experience is thinking you'll have left by midnight, but ending up calling a taxi at 6 a.m., when the grass is dewy and the street is quiet. Nodding off to sleep in the back seat, yawning with gratification.

THE JOURNEY
HOME

There is a reason plenty of feelgood films close with a completed trip; the end of a journey. A wide-angle shot of a bunch of festival-tired friends, heads leaning against one another; the close-up of a protagonist looking out of a plane window, a smile spreading across their face. Unlike so much that appears on screen, I know both these shots to be tangible and true.

A lot of people associate the good feeling of returning from a trip with switching the lights on, dumping luggage in the hall, putting the kettle on and breathing in the marinade smells of home. But that isn't coming home; that is arriving home.

No, what I love happens before that, the transition mixed with reflection. In the summer of 2019, I was at Glastonbury festival for work. I am extremely lucky in that I work with many of my best friends. After what I can only describe as the perfect five days, a few of us drove home.

Sometimes I would look over at my beautiful pal, her sleepy head rolling off the window, thinking about the new memories we'd just made. Or the four of us would rouse and have a singalong shot through with exhaustion; burst out laughing at a memory. It was the perfect coming home. The train journey on the way to the festival with a friend had been full of excitement (I also love going to places) and laughter; but the journey back is after a life changed, even if just a tiny bit.

I don't know what it is about watching countryside roll along on a solo train trip across Europe; piling out with mates at a service station for disgusting coffee (then sunbathing on a grassy bank at the edge of a car park); or that final butchering-of-a-language conversation with a congenial cab driver taking you back to the airport, that makes me contemplative and deeply satisfied.

Satisfaction, I think, in the pleasure of feeling grateful. Grateful for whatever one has experienced; whether it has been dancing at 4 a.m. with people you love, and then rising to the cool, bright morning; swimming in ludicrously clear waters; meeting people from around the world and hearing their stories; triumphing at the top of mountains. Gratitude towards life.

The overriding flavour of coming home is bittersweet, because often I don't want to. But it is knowing that nothing can last for ever, and that while it did last, it was glorious. Knowing that the fruit was not allowed to brown, no welcomes were outstayed. The most wonderful time, even with any imperfections, was had. So I am not sure home is where the heart is; I think the heart is in the bits in between.

ACKNOWLEDGE-
MENTS

A huge thank you to everybody involved in transforming two years' worth of columns into a lovely book. From initial phonecalls – while gulping tea and wandering around my garden – with Laura Hassan at Faber, to the brilliant and astute editing of Marigold Atkey. Great lunch pals and WhatsApp interlocutors, both. I am very lucky indeed.

Thank you to Kate Ward at Faber for helping to get me over the line, and Jonny Pelham for his marvellous cover design. Alex Bradshaw, Fred Baty and Mo Hafeez. Thank you to Yo – for her illustrations. To Hannah Turner and Niriksha Bharadia.

Major thanks to friends and colleagues at the *Guardian* who cared for the column and helped it thrive. Weekend editor Melissa Denes, and Saturday editor Clare Margetson, who, as well as being glorious humans and friends, gave me the go ahead when I brought the column idea to them (shout out too, of course, to J. B. Priestley himself, whose idea I nicked; and thank you to Hannah Mackay for introducing me to his book, *Delight*). To John Crace for his initial advice.

To the whole gang on the Weekend desk, but in particular those involved with Joy: Ruth Lewy and Joe Stone for their professional nous and general wonderfulness. To the subeditors who have saved me many times: Grainne Mooney, Georgia Brown, Catriona O'Shaughnessy, Andrea Chapman, Adrian Tempany, Frances Booth and Carrie O'Grady. To Katie Shimmon, Stephanie Fincham, Maggie Murphy and Pauline Doyle.

I wouldn't be at the *Guardian* without Tara Herman, Alan Rusbridger, Paul Johnson and Sheila Pulham, who truly did change my life. Thank you to Kath Viner and Jan Thompson for their ongoing support, and so many *Guardian* colleagues whose office company I miss dearly.

I have too many friends to mention here (she says, cockily), so I will just say I love you and you are the best. (Please assume this is a direct reference to you. Yes, YOU.)

During a once-in-a-century pandemic, a few people in particular have kept me sane. Thank you to Nigella Lawson for everything; the crumbles and so much more. Thank you to Polly Curtis for her barnstorming friendship and for interventions on Hampstead Heath and for always having my back. To Marina Hyde for the W2 walks and endless support. To Maya Wolfe-Robinson, Aditya Chakrabortty and Chris Godfrey for the latter also. Coco Khan, for picking me up from hospital on the hottest day of the year and then not murdering me when I managed to get us lost despite using a Satnav.

Tshepo Mokoena and Gwilym Mumford for being cheering, always. To Tim Jonze and Morwenna Ferrier for all of the Liverpool FC chat during a season of empty stadiums, and to Carys Ball, Sinead Morgan, Alix Davies, Ellen Hunter and Claire Barnett-Jones. To Eleanor Morgan for the voice notes and screengrabs and toast.

Many thanks go to Vera, Ruth, Eric for – somehow – putting up with me for thirty-one years; and to Graham, Evelyn, Sadie and Miles, who have put up with me for a much shorter time so let's see.

Thank you, so much, to my wonderful readers who are the loveliest people and whose emails, messages, social media interactions and letters are immensely lifting. You represent all that is good in the world and also have excellent taste.

Absolutely no thanks go to the man sat next to me in this cafe playing music out loud on his phone and endlessly jiggling his leg. No thanks whatsoever.